TRACKS ON THE FLORIDA TRAILS

by

Ned Potter
Illustrated by Larry Hill

To Harold Adkins with best regards from an old 99th Division survivor

Ned Potter

A Hearthstone Book

Carlton Press, Inc.　　　　　　　　　　New York, N.Y.

©1986 by Ned Potter
ALL RIGHTS RESERVED
Manufactured in the United States of America
ISBN 0-8062-2771-0

Dedicated to my dear granddaughter, Crystal.

ACKNOWLEDGMENTS

Where to begin with acknowledgments is difficult. I have surely been blessed to have had so many wonderful people share my life with me. Parents are where it all starts and mine certainly are to be acknowledged as ones who nurtured me and gave me room to grow in my own way.

Most of the narrative in *Tracks on the Florida Trails* is drawn from real-life experiences that I shared with my wife, Ceil, and my son, Ed. They have encouraged me and tolerated me as I recorded and wrote. For this I am grateful, but even more, I feel that our lives have been enriched beyond our understanding to have had these things happen to us together.

Beyond my immediate family, parents, wife and son, there are two friends to whom I owe a debt of gratitude. They are June Gallagher and Larry Hill. June did most of the rough typing and all of the final typing on the manuscript—a thankless task if there ever was one. She kept telling me that she enjoyed doing it so I continued handing her my "hen-scratched" originals. The fine art work was done by Larry. He kept saying that he was no artist, but I'll let the reader make the final decision on that point.

Going back in time, I wish to recognize four of my college professors as ones who were really great, in my estimation, and whose teachings went beyond the subject matter of the classroom. They are H.L. Bloomquist, Professor of Botany at Duke University; E.S. Ford, Professor of Botany at the University of Florida; N.E. Bingham, Professor of Education at the University of Florida; and Clara Olsen, Professor of Education at the University of Florida. It wasn't in the actual writing of "Tracks on the Florida Trails" that they helped, but rather it was the way they lived and acted along with what they taught that impressed my maturing mind. This is no easy judgment to make, either, for I have had some marvelous teachers in my life.

A source of assistance which I received and which I wish to acknowledge is the Bereau of Geology in the Department of

Natural Resources for the State of Florida. I wrote and asked questions on several occasions; they always responded to my queries. Many of the Geological facts which are incorporated in the various stories were corroborated or furnished by the bureau. Always, I have reported in the various stories my interpretation of what I thought they were telling me in their many letters and pamphlets.

In writing the chapter that deals with the channelization of the Kissimmee River, I referred to books and documents generously provided by the U.S. Fish and Wildlife Service and by the Jacksonville District of the U.S. Corps of Engineers. I am grateful to them for their cooperation.

Another state department that was equally helpful was the Florida Game and Freshwater Fish Commission. They gave me copies of research documents and guideline booklets that were most informative and useful in connection with stories about the Kissimmee River as well as phosphate mining in Florida.

I wish to acknowledge encouragement and assistance that I received from some old friends in the Florida Conservancy, a state department of The Nature Conservancy. Most didn't realize it at the time, but I received on the job training in principles of conservation from experts during my years as a Trustee and Editor of The Florida Conservancy Quarterly Bulletin. A more dedicated, hard working group of volunteers I have never known. Those whom I wish to acknowledge as vicarious contributors to *Tracks on the Florida Trails* are: George and Helen Allen, Alan and Vivian Bartlett, Steve Fickett, Fred and Pat Harden, Doris Mager, Ken and Helen Morison, and Wayne Wellman.

Finally, I would like to thank the University Presses of Florida, State of Florida University System for permission to quote from Sprague's "The Florida War" in Chapter I.

Ned Potter
Vero Beach, Florida
1985

CONTENTS

I	Tracks on the Trail	17
II	Freshwater Reefs	27
III	Miocene Floridians	36
IV	The Living Reef	45
V	Cretaceous Crustaceans	53
VI	From the Devil's Mill Hopper Down	63
VII	Kissimmee River Revisited	74
VIII	A Lost Cause	84
IX	From River-Pebbles to Land-Pebbles	92
X	Tabby on the Streets	104

Appendix 112
References and Recommended Reading 122
Index 125

FOREWORD
by Marjory Stoneman Douglas

One of the most important bad effects of the constantly increasing population of Florida is that the state is being filled up with people who know little about it and seem not to care. In truth, not so many books have been written about Florida, although it has the longest recorded history of any state in the Union. There are several very sound histories that are accurate and inclusive, but they are written as textbooks and lack a good deal of literary enthusiasm. The earliest book written by anyone about North America is an account by a young Spaniard named Fonteneda, who was captured by Indians and whose reprinted translation of his little book in Spain gave us the only book we have of the early days of the discovery of Florida. There is Dickinson's narrative, "God's Protecting Providence," written by a shipwrecked Jamaica merchant in the early 1600's, which is our only view of the east coast of Florida and the Indians of that time. There is the great book by Bartram which included travels in north Florida, that is our greatest classic. Since then there have been several little books written about the Civil War, by Mrs. Nicholas Eppes of Tallahassee, and of course the great books of Marjorie Kinnan Rawlings about the people of old Florida whom she met at Cross Creek, and by Zora Neale Hurston, about black people in Florida. My own book about the Everglades has become important since it discovered the Kissimmee-Okeechobee-Everglades basin in and its basic significance to the water supply of south Florida.

There maybe two or three other well-written books which I do not have in mind at the moment, but the great lack at the present day has been of a book so knowledgeable and so all-observant that it can serve to educate hordes of newcomers now and in the future. Thank goodness at last we have that book. It is written by Ned Potter, of Vero Beach, and called *Tracks on the Florida Trails*. I could not be more impressed with Mr. Potter's amazing knowledge of the whole state of Florida, his power of detailed observation and the range of his material. I cannot imagine there is anyone who knows more about the past of Florida historically, and the present from his own rich experience. It is the kind of book which should be in every bookstore and in all school libraries, and in the hands of both old-timers and newcomers who have never before found so much richness in a single medium-sized book. I forsee that there will be printing after printing for a long time, and new editions when this first one needs to be brought up-to-date in the future. He understands and writes vividly about the fundamental geology and geography, the weather, the plants, the birds and animals, and the population, which in this 400 years and more since the discovery has included people from all over the United States and many, increasingly, from the Caribbean and South America. The character of Florida, as he makes clear, will for untold years to come be conditioned as the gateway between the North and South American continents. In consequence, as he shows, it will have a significance not only in the relations between these continents, but in their economic, industrial, financial and demotic futures. He writes all this in the liveliest and most readable style imaginable. His own excitement and enthusiasm blossom from every sentence. His passion for Florida as the background of his own life emerges contagiously, to affect us all. It should produce a new burst of attention to this state, which has so much of the unique and valuable of the human, and humanly battered, and the infinite and unceasingly hopeful possibilities of the years to come. Let us hope that this new and most distinguished piece of writing will lead us to the wisdom necessary to make this Florida truly great.

PREFACE

Tracks on the Florida Trails has been about ten years in the making. The title chapter, Chapter I was written on an inspiration I received while I was on a hunting trip just West of Vero Beach, Florida. Things happened just as the story unfolds. I was walking along a trail and began to wonder how trails ever got started in the first place, so I began to speculate as I walked. I did most of the historical research about the Second Indian Wars after I returned home, however. "Fresh Water Reefs" and "Miocene Floridians" were the next two stories that I wrote. The two were written at a time when my son, Ed, and I were just nosing around. He had just been discharged from the service and we were trying to catch up on the time we had missed while he was gone. The former, now Chapter two, is about our exploration of rock reefs in the Everglades and Chapter III, "Miocene Floridians," tells of our discovery of a treasure trove of pseudomorphs while we were on a fishing trip.

These first three stories were written just for the fun of it with no idea that they might eventually become chapters in a book. Some friends read the early versions of them and encouraged me to think about writing more and then putting them all together as a collection of non-fiction short stories. About that time our son moved out on his own and my wife, Ceil, and I joined The Nature Conservancy and began attending the Florida Conservancy Quarterly conferences. "The Living Reef" (Chapter IV) was written after we returned from a conference meeting held on the Florida Keys; "Cretaceous Crustaceans" was also written as a result of another conference trip. In Chapter IV, I attempt to tell a little bit about reefs and their struggle for survival against the invasion of their domain by man. Chapter V is a story told exactly as it happened. The story is of our discovery (Ceil's and mine) of the discovery of oil in Florida. What prompted the story was our seeing our first Florida oil well.

The next four chapters (VI, VII, VIII and IX) are the result of some research that I did, regarding some places that I had been in time gone by. The places had impressed me greatly or the experience had been an important turning point in my life. "The Devil's Mill Hopper" is the actual name of a sinkhole just North of Gainesville, Florida. My first visit to the hopper was as a youthful student at the University of Florida. I have no idea how many times I crawled up and down those steep sloping sides, but at the time I had little knowledge of what sinkholes were or how they formed; I just enjoyed the break from classes. Later in life I read up on the subject, and Chapter VI is the result.

In Chapter VII, I try to describe the awful thing that has happened to the Kissimmee River. (At least I think it's awful to take a beautiful bit a nature and gouge it into the form of a big ditch.) The story in this chapter starts out describing the river as I knew it before channelization. There is a shift in time to the present and it is described as it is now. Then the story ends as two people discuss some of the plans to "restore" C-38 to river status. Restore is in quotes for a reason that will become apparent after you read "Kissimmee River Revisited". I don't know whether or not the reader has ever been lost in the woods, but I was once and it's a pretty sick feeling that you get in your gut. The experience made a large impressions on me and I vowed never to let it happen to me again. Chapter VIII, "A Lost Cause" tells of the experience and what I did about it.

Years ago, my family and I used to travel back and forth to Gainesville, Florida where we lived. The annual treks were for the purpose of furthering my education in summer school. Our trips took us right through what is known as the "highlands of Florida". Nobody can ride in that area without noticing the huge gouges in the Earth, the numerous milk-white ponds, and the great billows of smoke coming from the phosphate mines and processing plants. Finally, curiosity got the best of me as I pondered the hows and whys of the situation. "From River-Pebbles to Land-Pebbles" is a story about how the phosphate ore may have gotten where it is and why it is so important to us all.

The last regular chapter, "Tabby in the Streets," is a story that is told exactly as it happened. Ceil and I went to the quaint town of St. Augustine, Florida. It seemed that everywhere we went somebody was saying "... and this is made of Tabby!" We heard it as they told us about the fort, the buildings, the walls around the yards, and it seemed as though the streets were full of it. I just had to find out what the stuff is and why it was so important. Chapter X tells you of my findings.

The Appendix to *Tracks on the Florida Trails* is a summarization of the proceedings of an open forum that took place in an un-named town in Florida. The proceedings are heretofore unpublished but none the less interesting. I planned and conducted the forum as a result of reading a fascinating book, titled, "Limits to Growth," the publication of which was sponsored by the well known Club of Rome. In the book a world model is proposed utilizing the interrelationship of several variables vital to mankind. The uncontrolled use of non-renewable resources; increasing industrial production; pollution of our water, ground, and air; the so called population explosion; and so forth were all included in the model that they created. If things were to continue as they have progressed in the past, the old Earth couldn't take it much longer, they concluded.

The real quandary is that we people perceive progress as growth and we revere and pursue growth with a determined passion. If "it" isn't growing, then it's a failure and is dying. This rule applies to our country, each state, every town, all businesses, schools, and just about anything you can name in our modern industrial society. Such is not the case in nature, however. It may take several generations, but when a forest reaches maturity most of the growth occurs from within by replacement of worn out parts. It achieves a sort of equilibrium in which the soil, plants and animals arrive at a mutually beneficial "steady state." This is not just true in the biological sciences. Both the physical and biological sciences are filled with examples of how "nature seeks equilibrium" in a system. Anyway, I began to wonder what it would be like if man were to seek and establish equilibrium in his social and economic endeavors...and I wondered if anybody else ever thought about these sorts of things, outside the academic community, of course.

A group of business men and ladies from both the private sector and public sector were brought together to consider the hyphothesis. It wasn't easy to gather such a distinguished group together, I might add. I went to the local Chamber of Commerce to ask them to sponsor such a forum. It seemed to me at the time that with the chamber's support, I would have no problem getting the target group to cooperate. They—the Chamber of Commerce—would have no part of it! They would lose members if they even suggested such a thing. Perserverance paid off, however, and about one hundred middle-management people were assembled. In small groups they brainstormed the answers to five questions that were posed to break the ice and get them thinking along the desired lines. A group recorder reported the group reponses to the entire assembly afterwards; then there was a summary made and a copy of this was sent out to all participants. The Appendix reflects those results and they were quite enlightening.

One last comment seems necessary. *Tracks on the Florida Trails* and has been written in a personal style—the first person. Since I lived each story and then re-lived each as I wrote it, I saw no reason to write the book any other way. Likewise, the people mentioned in each story are real people. Their names have not been changed, although last names are not revealed. Their version of the stories contained herein might be interesting.

TRACKS ON THE FLORIDA TRAILS

CHAPTER I
TRACKS ON THE TRAIL

It wasn't a very pleasant feeling to be returning to camp without any game. I was particularly distraught since I didn't know how my hunting buddies had fared. If they had scored, then my "zip" would be the target of many jabs for some time to come. The thought of it made my bow heavier with each step. I guess every hunter tries to figure out what went wrong when they get skunked; I know I do. I also know you can't get something every time you get out in the woods, but somehow it's not much consolation.

I was running it all through my mind as I walked trying to figure out what I'd done wrong. My blind was built last summer; the boards were well weathered and the palmetto fans left few spots for turkeys to see in, especially from some distance away. I hadn't hardly moved for over three hours. As I recalled, what little I had moved was to chirp intermittently on my turkey caller. The blind was in a good location. I was sure of that because I'd gotten game there on two other occasions; infact, I'd heard turkeys fly up to roost over a nearby cypress swamp the night before. Everything had seemed right. Yet, dejected, I had finally gathered my things, circled the swamp and followed an obscure little game trail back to the Old Military Trail; and here I was headed for camp.

This seemingly innocuous dirt road runs roughly parallel to the East Coast of Florida and is some thirty miles inland at this point. It is indistinguishable from hundreds of others I've seen. Unlike the others, however, this one has a name and a somewhat unique place in American history. Now called the "Old Military Trail" by local folks, it is a small segment of what once was the "Lauderdale Trail". About the time of the Florida War, or sometimes called the Second Indian Wars, Major William Lauderdale and some of his comtemporaries built many stockade forts and supply depots throughout Florida and interconnected them with a number of trails. The purpose of it all was to help contain the Indians as well as to facilitate keeping out the white settlers until the indians were under control. Many of the trails had to be cut out of the primitive, untouched land; others, no doubt, were indian trails or old game trails made wide enough to accommodate a column of soldiers and their wagons. Reports of the commanders confirmed that the men frequently had to construct causeways and bridges through swamps and sloughs where it was too lengthy to go around.

This trail, named in honor of Major Lauderdale, began at Fort Dallas, now known as metropolitan Miami. The trail generally followed inland along the East Coast of Florida to Fort Jupiter. Proceeding Northwesterly from there, it eventually intersected with another East-West route known as the Ft. Pierce Trail. At the juncture of the two trails, a stockade fort was constructed. It was called Fort Lloyd and is now the site of the City of Okeechobee. The Lauderdale Trail then bore in a northerly direction to a place called Ft. Drum. Here it crossed an East-West trail that connected Ft. Vinton on the East Coast (Where Vero Beach is now located) with Ft. Brooke on the Tampa Bay. This trail connecting the coasts was known as the Capron Trail. From Ft. Drum, the Lauderdale Trail meandered northeasterly to Ft. Taylor, on the West bank of Lake Windner. This Northern terminus was just a few miles South of the present location of Cocoa, Florida. It was on their last segment of the Lauderdale Trail that I was walking.

Fort Drum was several leagues behind us now as I tried to imagine the hardships of a forced march to Ft. Taylor. Word had been passed down to my soldier of the past that they might make contact with Chief Alligator at any time, and he and his men were desperate for a victory. That the "Old Military Trail" looked very much then as it does now, I have no doubt. A weary soldier plodding along, head drooped from weariness, would have seen the deep ruts of wagon wheels where I now observe tire tracks. Between those ruts would have been footprints of horses, mules, or oxen-the beasts of burden of the times. I, too, see similar marks left by the cattleman's horse as he rounds up his steers. I do not see the bare footprints of the retreating Seminoles as my forebearer would, for they have long since been obliterated by the forces of man and nature. "It seems sad". I mused to myself,

"I've covered my soldier's tracks just as he did the Seminole's and just as the Seminole did the Ais". (The Ais were, of course, the first known human inhabitants of this portion of the peninsula we now call Florida.)

A path through the countryside is just as important to the indigenous wildlife as it is to man. It's probably a safe conjecture that the fauna, following their daily routine, made the trails first and the Indians took advantage of the fact that those trails were there and convenient to use. With no threat of danger, an existing path is frequently used and therefore, harder packed than the surrounding terrain. There is less obstruction and whoever (or whatever) passed there before most likely followed higher ground. It is part of the master plan for trails that each set of tracks assures another set of tracks will follow. I'd walked the "Old Military Trail" many times after the rain and seen where a great variety of wildlife had followed it. Frequent users are deer, wild hogs, raccoon, possum, rabbit, armadillo, and a variety of birds and reptiles.

One of the first things we do when we arrive at camp is to check the road for tracks. It tells us what's been in the area recently and lets us vicariously experience their presence (in case we don't get to actually see them). I don't think we've ever "checked for sign" that we haven't seen bobcat tracks. I think the cats have night patrol every night so they can pick up all the stray rabbits.

Another comforting reflection I've often had is that the trails which we follow today must surely be passing the same panorama of plant communities that they have for centuries. The "Old Military Trail" is relatively straight as it crosses the high and dry flatlands. It may deflect somewhat to bypass thick patches of saw palmetto or the dome-shaped cypress heads, but where there are few obstacles in the terrain, there are few detours in the trail. It's quite another story, however, as one approaches low marshy areas or sloughs. Here, the trail blazers saw fit to circle around and take the high ground...and the followers followed. From the vantage point of the perimeter one can see arrow root and pickerel weed reaching up above the surrounding rushes and sedges. Farther out from the center, in more casual water, gall berries and wax myrtles grow. Sometimes there are a few cypress and saw ferns interspersed around the edges or one may see Florida willows ringing the ponds. It all depends upon how wet it stays and what soil underlies the area.

Such a panoramic view isn't possible as you circle past a hammock or cut through a slough. Tall cabbage palms and live oaks festooned with spanish moss and bromiliads, so typical of the hammocks (or heads, as they are frequently called), are usually surrounded by a high curtain of palmettoes. Once, when I had penetrated the barrier, I sat on a moss-covered log to enjoy the primordal beauty. The trunks of the great oaks were too huge even to put my arms half way around them. The ground was a mass of fallen trunks all covered with mosses and ferns. Poking up through it all was the typical assortment of understory shrubs and vines all searching in their own particular fashion for the few rays of sunlight that filtered down from above. On occasion we have found orange and grapefruit trees growing in the heart of heads. They could be the result of seeds dropped by some hunter, but a far more intriguing concept is that the Seminoles used to plant citrus trees in the hammocks to assure themselves of some nourishment as they fought for their land. On this particular occasion, as I sat on my log, I thought it might be a good time to try out my new varmit call. In a very few moments a huge owl swooped quietly into the tree just over my head. If I hadn't

caught the motion out of the corner of my eye, I'd have never known he was there. I looked up and said "Hi". He glowered back quietly and forebodingly to the extent that I felt very uncomfortable. I got up and left him to his thoughts.

I was on the last leg of my trek back to camp, now, and had to follow the "Old Military Trail" as it crossed a wide creek bed...too wide to circumnavigate. Here, Major Lauderdale had had to build a causeway into the main run of the creek, construct a tressle bridge across it, and then build an elevated roadway out. Time has taken it's toll on the Major's project. Although the roadway remains fairly well intact, a small footbridge now stands where the tressle was washed away. From the outer limits of the run to the bed of the creek, the difference in elevation could not be more than eight feet. In basically flat Florida, however, such a subtle change in topography has a profound effect on the water table and the soil and, consequently, the flora. Where the trail is at the same level as the surrounding terrain, the palmettoes and pines give way to wax myrtle, dahoon holly, maples, oaks, lizzard tails and great patches of wild iris. In the spring, when the iris are in full bloom, the lavender blanket would make any gardener jealous. A water-filled mote on each side of the elevated roadbed reminds you that you are nearing the creek. Huge cypress trees and other hardwoods had to be cleared and ditches dug to build up the travelway. I think to myself, "It wasn't just shovels and axes that built this historical monument; the price included human life as well." Major lauderdale and his men fought mosquitoes, malaria, and the elements of nature while they were battling the Indians.

Perhaps the trials and tribulations of the Major's troops can be brought more clearly to mind in a report filed to the Adjutant General by another Indian fighter of the same war. According to John T. Sprague in his book, *The Florida War,* Col. Zachary Taylor wrote:

> This column, in six weeks, penetrated one hundredand fifty miles into the enemy's country, opened roads, and constructed bridges and causeways when necessary on the greater portion of the route; established two depots and necessary defenses for the same; and finally overtook and beat the enemy in his strongest position. the results of which movement and battle

have been the capture of 30 of the hostiles; the...(surrender of 150 other Indians and Negroes, the driving out of nearly 600 head of cattle and 100 head of horses)...besides obtaining a thorough knowledge of the country through which we operated, a greater portion of which was entirely unknown, except to the enemy." (1-213)

Two years later, in a subquent communique, the newly promoted General Taylor summarized progress made by the troops in Florida since first arriving there. He observed that fifty three forts or depots had been established, 848 miles of wagon trails had been cut through the wilderness, and 3643 feet of causeway and bridges were opened and constructed.

The sun was getting brighter again and the palmettoes undulating in the North wind signaled to me that I was only a short distance from camp. During these last few moments that I had to myself the feeling came over me that I, too, was a part of the master plan for trails. First a buck had walked here, then, perhaps a rabbit followed by an Indian stalking in hot persuit, and later maybe even Major Lauderdale, himself. Now a rancher, my hunting buddies and me are keeping the trail alive for those who will venture here tomorrow. I'd have to tell my partners about it all for they're as much a part of the master plan as I. I knew I'd have to let them have their hour of glory first, though. In camp, chiding a hunter who has been skunked always comes first; the serious stuff comes later while you are sitting around the camp fire.

(1-213)   Sprague, John T., *The Florida War* (Quadricentennaial Edition of the Floridana Facsimile Reprint Series-a Facsimile Reproduction of the 1848 Edition), University of Florida Press; Gainesville, Fla. 1964—P. 213

GLOSSARY FOR CHAPTER I

1. Ais Indians—the original tribe of Indians inhabiting Central East Coast Florida. The extent of their tribal grounds was roughly form the Cape Canaveral area, south to the St. Lucie Inlet and extended Westerly about halfway to the Kissimmee River. Like the Caloosa and the Timacua mentioned in Chapters IV and X, the AIS were hunters, fishermen, and farmers. When the Creek Indians were driven South from the Carolinas and Georgia these original inhabitants were decimated and the remnants of their civilization have almost disappeared.
2. Capron Trail—an east-west trail, used by colonial soldiers while fighting the Florida War (or the Second Indian War, as it is sometimes called.) It was an integral part of a network of trails and extended from Ft. Vinton on the East Coast (near where the modern city of Vero Beach is now located) through Fts. Bassinger and Drum to Ft. Brooke at the mouth of the Hillsboro River where it enters Tampa Bay.
3. Causeway—when a body of water must be spanned by a bridge, it is often prudent to build up the road bed out through the shallowest part of the water and just span the deepest part. Roadway extended in this fashion is called causeway.
4. Ft. Brooke— once situated near where Ybor City now sits, on the outskirts of Tampa.
5. Ft. Dallas—was originally located near the mouth of the Miami River, where it enters Biscayne Bay.
6. Ft. Drum—was a day's march along the Lauderdale Trail (Old Military Trail) going North from Ft. Lloyd. This portion of the trail followed a high sandy ridge which separates the Kissimmee River from the St John's Marsh. The trail, therefore, runs roughly parallel to the coast.
7. Ft. Jupiter—built near the mouth of the Loxihatchee River

near where the modern city of Jupiter now is.
8. Ft. Lloyd—built near the Northeast shore of Lake Okeechobee where Taylor Creek empties into the lake. The modern city of Okeechobee is near the original site of Ft. Lloyd.
9. Ft. Pierce—built near where the modern day city of Ft. Pierce is now located. It, along with Forts, Jupiter, Lauderdale, and Dallas, was built at the mouth of an inlet on the East Coast to try to stop gun runners from bringing guns and ammunition to the Indians. The Ft. Pierce Ttail was a trail that proceeded West from the fort and it intersected the Lauderdale Trail at Ft. Lloyd
10. Ft. Taylor—built on the Western shore of Lake Windner, about fifteen miles southwest of where the modern city of Cocoa stands.
11. Ft. Vinton—stood at the East treminus of the Capron Trail. The fort was located near where Vero Beach now stands
12. Fauna—refers collectively to the members of the animal kingdom, from the lowly amoeba to the striped zebra.
13. Flora—is the counterpart of fauna and refers collectively to members of the plant kingdom. All plants are included, from algae to the exotic and highly developed orchid.
14. Florida War—is also referred to as the Second Indian War. It wasn't until the hostile Seminole Indians could be brought under control, at the end of this war, that Florida became a state. The war ended in 1842, and Florida attained statehood in 1845.
15. Hammock—a hammock, or "head," as it is sometimes called, usually is associated with with an area of slightly higher elevation than nearby terrain. It is usually overgrown with broadleafed, hardwood trees and their associated understory.
16. Lauderdale Trail—in this story, the Lauderdale Trail is the same as the Old Military Trail. It ran Northerly from Ft. dallas to Ft. Jupiter and then angled Northerly to Ft. Lloyd where it intersected the Ft. Pierce Trail and continued Northwesterly to Ft. Drum where it intersected the Capron Trail and then angled slowly over toward the coast terminating at Ft. Taylor.
17. The Old Military Trail—in this story also known as the

Lauderdale Trail.
18. Seminole Indians—separated from the Creek tribe and fled to the South finding sanction in the Florida Territory. After banding together, they were called the Seminoles. Following their final defeat, most were resettled in Oklahoma, although some still remained in remote areas of Florida.

CHAPTER II
FRESHWATER REEFS

We decided that we had to see them from the air for ourselves. To be sure, we had thoroughly explored some rock reefs in the Everglades on foot; we had read about them in books; and we had seen photographs of them. When you look at a natural feature of the Earth from ground level or try to experience it vicariously through somebody else's words, it's just not the same. Whether it's an island or mountain or even a city, to see it from the air is to see it in its proper perspective in relationship to the features surrounding it.

A United States Department of Interior Geological Survey "Quad Map" shows a long, thin, green line arching to the west from Chekika State Recreation Area along with a miriad of green dots both to the North and South. That line represents one of the more accessible rock reefs and one that we had explored quite thoroughly. The green dots represent tree islands. "Let's rent a plane and take some of our own pictures," my son exclaimed.

"Why not?" I retorted....and with that we were on our way.

Soon we found ourselves accelerating down the runway of a nearby airstrip and gaining altitude over Marjory Stoneman Douglas' "River of Grass". As the horizon receded in all directions, I thought to myself, "It's a beauiful sight to behold." The first thing that caught my eyes was the reflection of the sun as it danced on the shimmering water and every so often, the sun's bright image would disappear into one of the numerous tree islands. My son and I had both seen it all before from a commercial plane. Under those circumstances, however, the view is perfunctory, if you're even aware of it. This was the real thing, though. Here we were, following our own flight plan, flying slowly at a fairly low altitude. Our purpose was to photograph and observe "that hogback" as the pilot had called it.

"There's Chekika!" That statement of fact accompanied by a nudge from the pilot reminded us of our mission. The plan was to circle Chekika State Recreation Area once and then fly West along the South edge of the "hogback" for about five miles. Then we had asked the pilot to swing around to the North side, fly back to Chekika and circle it once more before landing. All the while, my son was hanging out the door precariously by a strap and I was taking notes.

"These young kids don't seem to have any fear at all," I mused. I had the tough job of trying to oberve what he was photographing so we'd know what the sequence of pictures was later. It is difficult to discern the periferal landmarks when you are trying to take snapshots through the limited picture of a view finder. We thought that one shutter-bug backed up by an oberver would be the best way to handle the project.... and it seemed to work.

"Hogbacks," or rock reefs as they are more properly called, appear from the air as a long, narrow, straight or gently curving line of trees. If there were greater numbers and if they crisscrossed frequently they would remind you of the hedgerows in Great

Britain. This particular one we were flying over extended Westerly from Chekika State Recreation Area and gradually curved Northward until it disappeared over the horizon. There were intermittent breaks in the line, but there seemed to be no regularity on where they occurred. Since this particular reef was perpendicular to the flow of the Everglades current, we assumed that the gaps occurred wherever the water flow had eroded the surface away. The top does undulate slightly up and down, however, and some gaps seem to form at low points. Visible lengths seemed continuous for as much as a mile or more; other sections seemed to be a mere hundred yards or less in length. The width of a rock reef varies from about a dozen or more trees in most places to less than three of four trees.

The presence of hardwood trees and their accompanying dense undergrowth in the Everglades usually signals a subtle rise in the topography. Sometimes a clump of willows indicates the presence of a depression or a solution hole where organic acids percolating downward through the limestone have dissolved it away. The hole thus formed usually fills up with marl or alternating layers of marl and peat.

Solution holes tend to retain moisture through the dry season and support the growth of such marshy plants as pond apples, wax myrtle, saggitaria, pickerel weed, and a host of associated ferns. If you are afoot and you penetrate the surrounding growth ring, you will probably find a small muck pond, which may contain a "gator hole." In the soft ooze will be an abundance of animal tracks showing who ventured into the pond for a drink recently.

From the air, as well as the ground, solution holes are readily distinguished from tree islands. The latter appear as darker green solid "bumps" whereas solution holes are a light green ring of growth. On closer inspection tree islands, depending on their size, will have many of the same flora and fauna that tropical hardwood hammocks have. Here the underlying bedrock has mounded up somewhat higher than the surrounding "River of Grass". Perhaps capped by casehardened limestone and overlain by a protective layer of humus, the mounded area has not eroded away as rapidly as the nearby surface. The extra few inches to feet makes all the difference in the world.

During the dry season when the water is low, seeds may have

enough time to germinate and get their little heads high enough to remain above water during the rainy innundation. Then, if they don't get frozen back in successive winters, they may make it to maturity. The higher elevation not only provides a place for the unsprouted seeds to land, but it also acts as a catch-all for other organic litter carried downstream by the flow of water. The matter which accumulates soon reduces to detritus and adds itself to the soil's ability to support life. In no great hurry, a tree island thus formed, contributes its dome shape to the panorama of the Everglades.

Flying over the "Glades green" and viewing tree islands from the air, they appear as round bumps of green randomly set on a buffcolored carpet. In the summer, during the rainy season, the carpet is a saturated one, but during the "R" months, it is readily walkable for hikers so inclined to take on the saw grass and limerock outcropping. Be warned, however, cross-country walking in the Everglades is tough at its best. Many of the tree islands are oblong rather than round; some are even greatly elongated and drawn out into a long trail which points down stream to the flow of water. Size varies as well as shape. Only a few trees comprise some tree islands whereas, others are quite extensive. Once in a while, the larger islands exhibit spurs of growth radiating out from a central point and the longer spurs point more downstream. The miriad of tree islands west of Chekika State Recreation Area are divided by the rock reef which is what we wanted most to see.

During the high-water season, an aerial view of a "hogback" reveals another interesting feature that is not present otherwise. Since they are slightly elevated and where they run cross-wise to the sheet flow of water, they act as natural dam. Water is impounded to the North for as much as a quarter of a mile. Not readily seen from the air, however, but more easily discernable on the ground, is a slightly lower ground elevation on the downstream side of the rock reef. The difference in elevation can be as much as fifteen to eighteen inches, but generally it is less. This is , perhaps, due to porosity of the fresh water reef which allows the impounded water to seep slowly though. As it seeps through it carries dissolved organic acids which may speed up the erosion of the limerock base to the South. Also, unlike manmade dams, the rock reef is discontinuous and its top is uneven allowing water to flow both over the low points and through the gaps. All these variations provide a number of different "mini-habitats" within the main ecosystem of the Glades.

Upstream from a rock reef, the impounded water provides a quiet pond inhabited by scattered cocoplum trees growing on a mat of periphyton. A hundred yards in width, these ponds contain few of the grasses and spike rushes so typical of the Glades. To the South it's quite a different story. As water seeps through the permiable dam, it carries solute and particles which produce an organic sediment bathed slowly by an enriched, slightly acid solution. In this medium can be found the more typical "Glades" flora such as saw grass and spike rush and, close to the reef, even hardwoods. Viewed from the air these areas appear wider than the rock reef actually is and dark streamers of vegetation can be seen, almost making you think of Spanish Moss hanging from the branch of a tree. The festoons offer a distinct contrast to the clear ponds entrapped to the North.

Between the emergent segments of the reef, there are washouts that begin well to the North. They run through a narrow break in the "dam" and open up again on the South side. Viewed from the air, they appear as ponds formed into an hour-glass shape. On the ground there is a readily discernible current at the nexus which accelerates erosion of the underlying rock. Normally, water flow in the Everglades is measured in inches per hour and is almost undetectible to the naked eye. The flow is not only slow because of the flatness of the land; it is also impeded by the dense growth of plants as well as the rough, irregular surface. Walking across one of these washouts, therefore, is quite a unique experience. The water not only gets deeper, but you can feel the push of the current against the side of your legs.

As we neared the end of our flight, I jotted down in my notes as my son recorded photographically a relatively recent feature of this particular rock reef. It was one that we had not expected to see. What surprised us was the criss-crossing of roads of a new subdivision! The reason we were surprised was that all the land between Chekika State Recreation Area and Everglades National Park had been at one time designated by Dade County as "Preservation Zone" ... i.e. to remain in its natural state and not to be developed by man in any way. Not only is this an environmentally sensitive area, but it is part of the recharge area of the Biscayne Aquifer where Dade Countians get their drinking water. Now, with development being allowed, the drinking water will soon be contaminated by septic tanks, fertilizers, herbicides, insecticides, and who knows what else. Besides all that, roads with their borrow ditches, bull dozers, and bright yellow trucks just did not fit the scene we expected.

The flight plan called for us to circle Chekika State Recreation Area one time before landing. As we did my son and I both decided that we "needed that." We were both elated by the picturesque view of the rock reef and its accompanying tree islands and we were dismayed to discover the sanctity of the preservation zone had been broken. There aren't many places on Planet Earth where rock reefs can be found. They are a geological and geographical oddity that is apparently unique to Bryozoan Limestone. Not always observed in that type of rock, they are never found in other kinds.

One has but to experience a "hogback" to wonder where they came from and how they were formed. In all truth, there has been much more speculation and observation of them than empirical research. One of the more educated guesses is that rock reefs represent the existence of old shore lines which occurred in geological times gone by. Whatever their origin, they are an integral feature of Florida's Everglades and one of its natural resources which can never be replaced.

GLOSSARY FOR CHAPTER II

1. Biscayne Aquifer—a layer of porous limestone that under lies the coastal ridge on which the city of Miami is built. Since it slopes upward to the West, it comes near the surface out in the Everglades. Because it is porous, it absorbs rain water during the rainy season. The water moves Easterly by capillary action as well as by flowing through fissures in the limestone so that it, too, lies underneath the city and is available as the primary source of drinking water for all of Metropolitian Miami.
2. Bryozoan Limestone—was deposited during the Pleistocene period and is named after minute forms of animal life called Bryozoa. The Bryozoa were plentiful when the limestone was formed and their lime encrustation contributed to the sediment from which this limestone was formed.
3. Detrius—loose material, such as small particles of rock and shell and other organic matter, that has been reduced to its small size by the process of erosion.
4. Ecosystem—very briefly, an ecosystem consists of all the inter-related plants, animals, and soils of an area. The flora and fauna must be indigenous to the area so that they are classed as being typical of the area.
5. Fauna—see Glossary for Chapter I.
6. Flora—see Glossary for Chapter I.
7. Hammock—see Glossary for Chapter I.
8. Hog Back—a common name for a rock reef. See definition for rock reef in this glossary.
9. Humus—the partially decomposed organic material that becomes incorporated into the soil. As leaves fall and as plants and animals die, bacteria begin to decompose their remains; the material thus formed enriches the soil and makes it more capable of supporting other living organisms.
10. Limestone—a sedimentary type of rock that is formed from the sediment that settles to the bottom of the ocean. The

sediment usually consists of a thorough mixture of limey mud, shell fragments, and sand. The mixture is sometimes referred to as micrite.
11. Marl—a "clayey" type of soil that has shell fragments and other calcareous material mixed in with it.
12. Muck Pond—a soil with a great amount of organic material (detritus, humus, etc.)mixed into it. A muck pond is one with muck soil for a bottom. Quite often the organic material is so fine that it ramains suspended in the water rather than settling to the bottom and it gives the water a blackish look.
13. Periphyton—in the Everglades, the sediment in the shallow water often has fresh water algae growing profusely in the detritus. The felt-like mat that forms from the algae holding the detritus loosely together is called periphyton. It can accumulate over the years and become quite thick. It is always very slippery when you try to walk on it.
14. Peat—as it is used here in this story, it refers to the peat found in the Everglades. It is formed when there is an accumulation of partially decomposed plant material that has remained in a submerged (under water) state for a long time.
15. Percolate—percolation is the downward movement of water through the soil and porous limestone. Percolating water picks up acids dissolved from the atmosphere and from the decaying organic matter in the soil. As the acidic water percolates through the limestone, fissures, cavities, and crevices in the limestone become enlarged because the acid dissolves the limestone.
16. Preservation Zone—an area of land designated in a county land use plan as an area where "No development is permitted which would remove or displace organic soils, native vegetation, or endangered species of wildlife."
17. Rock Reef—a naturally occurring reef-like structure which may be found in the Everglades of Florida. It is generally an abrupt rise in the surface that may extend for miles. A rock reef is usually not too wide across the top and its rise may only be a few inches to a foot or more. The "hog back" may be continuous for a considerable distance or it may be broken into sections. Since it is higher than the surrounding

terrain, it is usually overgrown with typical hammock-type growth.
18. Solution Hole—formed when slightly acidic water dissolves away limestone near the surface. (See definition for percolate in this glossary.) When this occurs it leaves a depression or, maybe, an hourglass-shaped hole in the limestone. The hole/depression may be three or so feet in diameter or it might be as much as 30 to 40 feet across. Often solution holes fill up with detritus, marl, muck, and peat and that is carried along by the flow of water. When this happens the hole may become a fertile base for swampy plants to grow, such as willows, pond apples and so forth.
19. Tree Island —as explained in the definition of rock reefs, any small rise in the topography of the Everglades may be a place where broad-leafed, hammock-type plants can grow. When such a slight mounded area becomes the home of tropical flora, it appears as an island in the middle of the surrounding sea of saw grass.

CHAPTER III
MIOCENE FLORIDIANS

A forgotten page, or little known one, from the biography of Florida was recreated for my son and I one day when we least expected it. We were taking a fishing break after a long, cold wait in our tree stands. No prize bucks had passed our way and we each had descended downhearted and stiff from inactivity. Many times before, under similar circumstances, we had walked back to our camp, gotten our fishing gear, and gone to a nearby canal to fish. Of course, when the solunar table says the game is inactive, and probably bedded down, the fish aren't feeding either. We go fishing anyway though, because it gives us a chance to stretch our legs...and you never know when a big lunker is going to try to take your bait away from you.

Canal fishing in Florida is really quite simple if you don't have a boat. You just walk along the bank casting across to the little coves and lily pads on the other side. A weedless hook is almost a necessity so we use plastic worms with the hook looped back through, but not quite all the way. Intent as I was, looking for a good spot to the cast to, something under my feet caught my eye. "It's just a rock!" I said to myself. But this particular rock had a peculiar shape to it and that's what caught my eye. Its peculiarity was that it was not the typical nondescript, irregularly shaped rock. Quite to the contrary, it was formed in neat tight spiral like a huge snail. Yet, I could tell it wasn't a snail because it was the color of all the other rocks. Then, too, it was too large to be a fresh water snail and we were fifty miles from the gulf. As I picked it up, the spiral shape and the striations on its surface became more evident. "Why, it looks just like that giant tun shell that my wife found on the beach last summer," I said to myself aloud. Hastily, I glanced around to see whether Ed had heard me. He kids me a lot about talking to myself, but this time I was safe since he wasn't in sight.

Like space, time is but another dimension. In a sense, Ed and

I had gone backward in one while traveling forward in the other as we traversed the southern tip of Florida. We had left Miami early the previous morning and arrived at camp about noon. Although the highway was relatively flat, the underlying layers of limestone slope gently downward to the east and South. Thus, traveling westerly, we saw increasingly older limestone outcropping. It changes from recently formed Pleistocene limestone near the East Coast to older Bryozoan Limestone, underlying the Everglades and then to Tamiami Limestone beneath the surface of the Great Cypress Swamp.

About twenty five million to thirty five million years ago, the Tamiami Limestone was formed. All of Florida, South of what is now called Okeechobee, was inundated by the Miocene Seas, and penninsular Florida consisted of a much narrower and shorter spit of land than now exists. The sea floor, sloping away from the Miocene beaches, supported a variety of marine life not too dissimilar from what we know today. The very spot where I had picked up my "rock" was once under some fifty feet of water.

Just a few short years ago some dragline operator had unwittingly unearthed the unmarked grave of this Miocene Floridian. A few minutes ago I had just as unwittingly stepped upon its ancient remains. Startled for a moment at my transgression, I said, "Other people have walked here too." Looking around and seeing more shellshaped "rocks" than the eye could count I said, "Why there's no telling how many graves have been desecrated or how far their remains have been scattered ". I felt a little bit better knowing I wasn't the only one who had disturbed them.

I spent some time sifting through the "rocks". There were quite a number of different marine forms represented there. I recognized "rocks" that looked like oysters, clams, turkey wings, lion paws and Venus shells. Other looked similar to the spiral shells such as the giant tun, conus and olive shells. There were also replicas of sand dollars, sea worms and lamp shells to serve as evidence that there were non-mollusk marine animals represented. (Later at home, a hand lens revealed the intricate lacy designs of corals, sponges, bryozoans, and lime-producing algae. I also discovered that some four hundred ancient species have been identified and named.)

The "fossils" I was looking at and collecting are called Pseudomorphs. They aren't really fossils in the true meaning of the word. Rather, they were moulds, formed in the shape of the shell where the animal itself was the pattern for the mould. These particular ones that I was looking at were the remains of ocean bottom dwellers—either slow-moving or burrowing animals. Some grew attached to rocks or to the hard parts of other animals. Benthos forms of life, they were subject to rapid entrapment in the shifting sediment of the ocean floor. In addition, they had to produce some hard structure of their own so they wouldn't be crushed in the burial process. Since they lived at about ten fathoms, they are different than what might have lived in the beach and tidal zones of the Micocene period. After all, the conditions in deeper waters would be cooler, darker, and less agitated by wave motion. Pressure, oxygen content, and salinity would also be determining factors just as they are today.

As I was running all these ideas through my mind, I set about the task of searching diligently for both good specimens as well as a variety of representative species. Some of the pseudomorphs appeared to look like the outside mould of a shell; others looked like an inside mould; a third category looked exactly like the shell must have looked twenty five to thirty five million years ago. I threw my rod and reel aside, and as a child in a dimestore, started looking everywhere at once. Also as a child might, I had soon collected more "rocks" than a man and two horses could carry. Wanting to share my treasure trove with my son, I hollered, "Ed"!

"Right here!" he said from the other side of the canal bank. "Dad, look what I've found. These rocks look just like shells , and they're not fresh water shells either. How could they have gotten here?"...and how could rocks get to look like shells?"

I was mulling it all over in my own mind as he asked his questions. There has persisted, in years gone by, the idea that sediment was transformed into rock only under extreme pressure and heat. More recently, however, there is good reason to believe that limestone formation can occur under quite "ordinary" conditions. An over simplified explanation begins with the accumulation of animal and plant sediment on the bottom of the ocean—a collection of minute fragments of the skeletal remains of microscopic organisms such as protozoa, bryozoa, foraminifers, corals, sea urchins, shell fish of all sorts, and "limestone producing" algae. Fragmentation probably occurs as the remains of the once living organisms are "stirred" by the motion of the water. Such sediment, when it builds up over hundreds of thousands, even millions, of years, can become hundreds of feet deep. In some instances the land could be warping downward at about the same rate that the sediment is being deposited and the actual depth of the water could remain relatively static. At other times the underlying rock could be warping upward as the loose, limey material accumulates. Apparently, the latter conditions have prevailed in Florida since the beginning of the Miocene Epoch, or for about the last twenty eight million years.

Step two of the formation of limestone involves exposure of the microchrystalline ooze (sometimes referred to as Micrite) to a subaerial, fresh water environment. That is to say, the bottom of the ocean must emerge as land above sea level. The lower layers don't necessarily have to be exposed to air for they will eventually succumb to exposure by fresh water as it leaches down from above. The important thing in the process is the presence of fresh water and the substances dissolved in it.

Rain falling onto the surface and seeping through the porous "neo-limestone" leaches away cement-inhibiting materials and at the same time calcite, a cement-forming material, leaches into the sediment. It is the replacement of materials that acts as a catalyst to finalize the formation of limestone, or lithification as it called. The porosity of the end product of the process is dependent upon the materials that went into its making, but in most cases the limestone is somewhat less porous than the micrite from which it was formed. There is, therefore, a slight volume change associated with the process.

For limestone to contain objects which have the appearance of a shell—be it inside mould or outside mould—is now more readily understood. A mollusk can easily become entrapped and burried in the soft, oozy bottom. Hydraulic action over a considerable period of time can cause the shell to completely fill with the muddy material and replace the soft tissue of the animal within. In effect there would then be a shell suspended in the surrounding medium. Little, if any change occurs until the sediment with its embedded shells (and any other remnants so entrapped) is elevated to a subaerial, fresh water environment. Only then does lithification, or hardening, or cementation, occur. There is evidence that limestone formation can occur in a submarine environment, but under conditions other than those just described.

Porosity of limestone and the concomitant seepage of rain water down through it are important to the formation of pseudomorphs. As the water percolates downward it carries dissolved acids from the atmosphere and from the prolific decay of rotting vegetation. This action over extended periods of time, and we're talking about millions of years, may cause the originally formed shell material (called aragonite, which is the same as calcite, but in a different crystalline structure) to dissolve away completely. The surrounding limestone, however, retains the shape of the shell that was embedded in it. This would leave both an outside and an inside mould of the shell each separated by the space left behind. Even more astounding is the fact that the space vacated by the shell can be filled up by more rock material being brought down in solution from above.

With the leaching downward of dissolved minerals through the porous limestone, the upper layers become donors of the dissolved aragonite to the lower layers. One more change usually occurs. When the original shell material dissolves and then later recrystallizes, it reforms its crystaline structure. That is to say on the molecular level, when aragonite goes into solution it precipitates out as a more stable compound called calcite-or calcium carbonate.

I was explaining all this to my son as we walked back to our camp. "It's as though we have seen just a few seconds of a long motion picture film. We can pick up a few more seconds in another layer of rock and a few more from somewhere else. Finally, if we could collect enough segments and put them together in the proper sequence, we could write a fairly accurate biography of Florida," I said. I was pretty proud of the analogy and thought I had made a point with Ed.

"By the way, Dad," he retorted, "weren't you talking to yourself again back there?" I don't think he heard a word I said, but after all we were out hunting and fishing and not in a classroom.

GLOSSARY FOR CHAPTER III

1. Algae—algae are fairly simple members of the plant kingdom. They do not have true roots, stems, leaves or flowers. They are mostly aquatic living in both fresh water and the sea.
2. Aragonite—the name of the material from which the shells of mollusks are made. Since it is derived from organic materials secreted by the animal making the shell, it has a different crystalline structure than calcite but the same chemical elements occur in each. (See Calcite in this Glossary)
3. Benthos—referring to organisms that live on the bottom of the ocean. They may be attached to something or they may crawl on the bottom or burrow in it. They may spend a small portion of their lives as free swimmers, however, the vast amount of time is on the bottom.
4. Bryozoa—a group of diminutive animals that look, at first glance, like mosses. They are aquatic, though, rather than land- based. Under a microscope they resemble the polyp of a coral except the bryozoan has a chitinous covering and the coral polyp does not. Bryozoan colonies seem to grow on most anything that lives in the water. They are found growing on rocks, shells, sea weed and so forth.
5. Bryzoan limestone—see glossary for Chapter II
6. Calcite—also known as calcium carbonate has the chemical formula $CaCO_3$ which means that calcium, carbon, and oxygen are part of its makeup. Calcite is an important constituent of limestone.
7. Calcium Carbonate—See Calcite
8. Catalyst—a chemical substance that speeds up or slows down a chemical reaction without actually entering into the reaction itself, or at least it remains unchanged after the reaction has been completed.
9. Coral—we commonly refer to the hard, stony structure that we collect for specimens as being coral. The structure that we admire so much is secreted by a microscopic, anenome-like animal called a polyp. Technically, the two together—the animal and its home—are living coral.

10. Foraminifers—part of a large group of animals that includes the amoeba. Foraminifers differ from the amoeba, however, by having a hard chitinous outer covering.
11. Fossil—either the hard, petrified remains of an animal or the replica of the animal that has been produced by natural processes. There are fossil remains of plants, too, but the key in both animal and plant fossils is that the evidence has been preserved by some process of nature.
12. Giant tun—a large snail-like or conch-like mollusk whose shell is formed into a spiral shape.
13. Leaching—a process whereby minerals in the soil or porous limestone are dissolved in percolating rain water and carried down through the soil and limestone with the water as it soaks in.
14. Limestone—see glossary for Chapter II
15. Lithification—the name given to the cementing process where sediment becomes stone.
16. Micrite—another word for microcrystalline ooze. (See microcrystalline ooze in this glossary.)
17. Microcrystalline ooze—this substance is the sediment from which limestone is formed. See also *Limestone* in the Glossary for Chapter II.
18. Miocene—the Miocone Epoch (or age), is a geological period of time that goes back twenty eight million years ago and ended about twelve million years ago.
19. Neo-limestone—a term applied to newly forming limestone.
20. Percolate—see glossary for Chapter II.
21. Pleistocene—the Pleistocence Epoch (or age), is a geological period that began about three million years ago and lasted for about two million years. Pleistocene limestone was formed during this Epoch.
22. Precipitate—See Stalactite in glossary for Chapter VI.
23. Protozoa—a term used for one-celled organisms.
24. Pseudomorph—a type of fossil where none of the original animal has been preserved. The soft part has decayed away; the hard part has dissolved away and been replaced with minerals that have leached down to fill up the empty space.
25. Sedimentary rock—formed from material that settled to the bottom of the ocean in the form of fine sediment such as mud or sand.

26. Sponge—as in the case of coral, the spongy material that we squeeze in our hands was once the home of a tiny little one-celled protozoan-like creature that is called a Choanocyte. Technically, both the animal and its home comprise a living sponge.
27. Subaerial environment—one that is exposed to atmospheric weathering, and its surface is therefore above sea level.
28. Submarine Environment—as the name implies, a Submarine Environment includes everything below sea level.
29. Tamiami limestone—formed from sediment that was deposited on the ocean floor late in the Miocene Epoch or from about fifteen million years ago till about twelve million years ago.

CHAPTER IV
THE LIVING REEF

How one perceives a living coral reef depends on their point of view. If you were a polyp, you'd look at it from the inside; it's your home. You built it. From within the calcareous structure, your tiny, wriggling body would stretch little tentacles out to catch other microscopic marine forms as they drifted by on the ocean currents. The small stony cup which is your home is but one of many in a colony, and its hard skeleton-like form protects you from all but a few preditors. If, on the other hand, you happen to be an anemome or an urchin or a sailor's choice, you would still think of the reef as your home, but in a different way from the polyp.

You might attach yourself to the reef and catch your dinner much as the polyp does....or you might crawl or dart around the numerous branches and grottoes. Why you would dart would depend on whether you are chasing dinner or being chased. In any case, the reef would be your host and it would furnish food and shelter to you as well as to throngs of other flora and fauna of the sea. In a very real sense, you would be a part of the living reef system even though you were apart from it.

On nearby Cays, others might consider the reef a part of their home too. The Caloosa Inidans, who inhabited the Florida Keys for thousands of years before the advent of Spanish explorers, are a case in point. They were excellent sailors and swimmers who dove for conchs, turtles, crawfish and crabs; they also fished from their dugouts as they paddled above. Together with wild berries, melons squash and other native edible plants, the Caloosa dined well. The islands furnished wood for boats, tools and homes. Leaves and fiber for thatching and clothing were available as well. That there was also an abundance of game roaming the keys is evidenced by bones of deer, bear and rabbit in their middens, or old settlements. The mounds of oyster shells are mute evidence, however, as to the caloosa's favorite food. For them the living reef and cays furnished an idyllic life.

Little did the Caloosa realize, nor did they probably care, that many of the cays they inhabited were old reefs formed hundreds of thousands of years ago. As the islands changed hands from the Caloosa to the Spanish conquistadors to the English to the likes of Black Caesar and Jean LaFitte, knowledge of the origin of the cays was unimportant compared to survival. When Henry Flagler arrived on the scene, however, he dreamed of extending a railroad from the mainland all the way to Key West, hoping to provide a main link in a new trade route down the East Coast of the United States, through the Panama Canal to the Pacific Ocean. In an effort to obtain rock for railroad beds and for riprap for his causeways, Flagler discovered that the Northern Keys had a solid coral rock foundation. One of the highest elevations in the entire overseas route was at Windley Key, adjacent to Plantation, and it was there that he established a stone quarry. From it, Flagler mined huge slabs of coral rock.

Presence of this coral rock at one of the high points of the keys portends another story that was enacted eons ago. For dry land to be based on coral rock, it must have been under water at one time. That the Keys were submerged in the past cannot be doubted. There is too much evidence to substantiate the fact. Movements of the earth's crust are commonly known. Those who have not experienced an earthquake have surely read of the many recent ones around the world and, possibly, even contributed food or clothes to help those who have. There is powerful evidence to substantiate the theory that huge platelike land masses on the earth's surface are migrating or shifting position realtive to each other and heaving up whole mountain chains as well as creating whole new valleys in the sea floor. If the amount of water can be considered to be constant, its level would be sure to go up and down with the changing capacity of the ocean basins.

Another very well real hypothesis that the sea level has risen and fallen is that the volume of water is changing and has changed in times gone by. Glaciation is known to have occurred from twenty to seventy thousand years ago. Infact, it is also known that there have been at least four glacial periods in the last half million years and that glacial activity may be a cyclical phenomenon associated with alternate cooling and warming of the Earth. As it gets cooler, more and more of of evaporated water falls as snow during the arctic and antarctic winters. Water thus trapped in the form of snow and ice is removed from the ocean but not from the total earth system. It still remains as an intregal part of the water cycle. The earth's cooling produces a glacial period. With the advent of a warming trend, the interglacial period, the polar caps would begin to melt and to fill up the ocean's basins. Land masses, which were relatively static in their movement up and down (from other forces) would experience an inundation of sea water. It has been estimated that if all the ice on Earth today were to melt, the water level would rise almost two hundred feet.

Most likely, both forces—glacial activity and shifting plates of the Earth's surface—have combined to cause sea level to rise and fall during recent geologic times. North from the Florida Keys about three hundred miles, there is positive evidence. The highway from Gainesville to Cedar Key follows across rolling, sandy hills that are very reminiscent of old sand dunes and sandy beaches. An ancient seashore in that area must have been inland by fifty to seventy five miles from where the current shoreline is. By the same logic and similar evidence old, inundated shorelines have been identified from soundings several miles out in the Gulf of Mexico. Explanations about why oscillations of the sea level have occurred are not readily available in the form of empirical evidence. Some attempts have been made to link intermittent glaciation to solar radiation and astronomical theories regarding the evolution of stars in general and of our sun in particular. Be that as it may, alternate warming and cooling of the Earth has occurred and with it rising and falling seas.

"What has all this got to do with the living reef system?" you may be asking yourself. "How did we get from polyps to photons in such a few short paragraphs?" Henry Flagler probably didn't give much thought about how a reef could have formed ten or fifteen feet above water, but then he may have pondered for quite some time on it. What we do know is that Flagler completed his overseas railroad. In so doing, his men built about twenty miles of causeway, thirty seven bridges, and one hundred twenty eight miles of railroad track from the mainland of Florida to Key West. We also know that the extinct reef which is now exposed at the Windley Key Quarry played an important role in the accomplishment. For the first time a reef was not viewed as a "home", but rather it was a thing to be exploited....to be carved up in undignified chunks and hauled off. The reef that Flagler quarried was not the living reef system, though; it was the ramains of an ancient reef built a hundred thousand years ago and one that has long since been left high and dry by receding seas.

Prior to the building of the overseas railway, the only access to Florida's keys was by boat. Isolation and the insects eliminated all but the hardiest of settlers. Flagler's train, and later the overseas highway, made development more feasible and that development was not long in arriving. Construction of the railroad tracks was begun in 1905 and completed in 1912. Destroyed by a hurricane in 1935, it was soon replaced by the overseas highway. The in-migration of settlers was further enhanced in 1941 by the coming of a fresh water pipeline and the building of an electrical power plant. Thus, people have been establishing residence in the Keys almost continually since the turn of the century.

That the living reef suffered in the transition should never be doubted. It was torn asunder by dredges, anchors, and souvenir hunters. Worse than that was the cloudy slit from construction. Turbidity of the water from dredges reduces the amount of light available to marine life forms. Such a situation is intolerable to the living reef system and in some places as much as eighty percent of the organisms died or were destroyed. Thankfully, there were a few sensitive people who recognized what was happening and pressed for laws to halt the degradation.

Before the reef was completely destroyed, but not a minute too soon, legislation was passed in Florida to establish the John Pennekamp Coral Reef State Park and still later, the Federal Government through the Department of Commerce extended the State Park calling it the Key Largo Coral Reef Marine Sanctuary. The combination of the two actions offered protection to an area twenty miles long and eight miles out into the Atlantic Ocean.

Creating a State Park and a Federal Marine Sanctuary was step one in halting destruction of the most extensive living reef system of the United States. Subsequent laws were passed to protect the outer, reef all along the Keys, but what brought about the change in perception? Marine studies had established that a living reef performs three important functions: First, they provide important protection against storm damage to the shore; Second, they are an important source for sand production for beaches: Third, reefs form the basis for an intricate ecosystem and are essential for many forms of marine life to exist....including several species of game fish. Indeed, now reefs are viewed as so important to the Keys, that ways are being sought to replace the losses of the early 1900's.

Under serious consideration is the possibility of "transplanting" and "cultivating" reef building organisms making it possible to accelerate growth in some of the sections that have been destroyed. If left to nature alone, the rebuilding process might take hundreds of thousands of years, for reef growth is extremely slow. For example, branching corals such as staghorn and elkhorn may only grow as much as two or three inches per year; an average dome-shaped, or brain coral, may take as much as one to two hundred years to become a few feet in diameter. Surely, the huge slabs of coral rock mined by Mr. Flagler must have been thousands of years in the making.

One of the things modern marine scientists desperately need to study reef growth is to be able to study cross-sections and longitudinal-sections of a reef. To cut out sections of the living reef system, however, would be to destroy the very thing they are trying to save. What a dilemma! Flagler's quarry solved the problem. Since the quarry represents about ninety seven thousand years of growth from its top to its bottom, students have a natural outdoor laboratory. In addition, the fossil coral of the quarry is about eighty percent pure coral and it contains twenty eight species of the thirty seven species of coral and that have been identified on the outer living reef. The great cuts made both lengthwise and crosswise provide the sections needed for examining how the ancient reef came to be. What, at first glance, appeared exploitive of the fossil reef is now viewed as a blessing in disguise.

It is apparent where living reef systems are concerned that inhabitants of a coral reef community-including those who are a part of it and those who are apart from it-are a community in the full meaning of the word. They live together and are inter-dependent upon each other. The Caloosa Indians seemed to recognize the fine balance of nature that existed within the physical world around them......and that balance included them. There was a spiritual relationship as well, where each physical object-the reef, a tree, the ocean, the cays-had form and function to be revered for itself. Modern, "civilized„ man has somehow dissociated himself, spiritually, from the world of nature and we may have lost something in the process.

GLOSSARY FOR CHAPTER IV

1. Calcareous—referring to a structure or rock made from calcite. (Se Calcite in Glossary for Chapter III.)
2. Caloosa Indian—like the Ais (see Ch. I), a tribe of the original Apalachee Indians that inhabited peninsular Florida. Their tribal area was the Southwest Coast from the Tampa area South to the tip of Florida and West to around the Lake of Okeechobee area.
3. Causeway—see glossary for Chapter I
4. Cay—just another word for a key. The Florida Keys were originally called cays by the early settlers.
5. Coral rock—what we now call coral rock, used to be, at one time, living coral; it now forms the bedrock for many of the upper keys, from Key Largo to the Matacumbees.
6. Fauna—see glossary for Chapter I.
7. Flora—see glossary for Chapter I.
8. Fossil—see glossary for chapter III.
9. Glacial Period—a geological period of time when the earth was cooler than it is at present, and because it was cooler, the polar caps were accumulating increased amounts of ice from year to year. The ice didn't have time to melt through the shorter summer before more ice would begin to form. At the same time, due to the concomitant loss of water, the ocean level was going down.
10. Interglacial Period—the counterpart of a glacial period. The earth was getting warmer, the polar caps were melting faster than the ice could build up, and the sea level was rising.
11. Midden—the site of an old Indian village, especially a village of the original Apalachee tribes. Almost always piles of oyster shells are found here. Few artifacts remain, however, because of collectors and because the tropical climate destroys them so fast.
12. Photon—a unit or particle of light energy; used in this

instance to refer to sunlight.
13. Polyp—the organism that "builds" the stony structure which we commonly call a reef. (See also *Coral* in the glossary for Chapter III.)
14. Riprap—used by engineers to prevent soil erosion on the sloping banks of causeways for bridges. Rainfall and wave action would undercut the roadbed of a causeway without it. In modern times we use poured concrete or sloping layers of bagged concrete. Mr. Flagler used huge slabs of coral rock to lay on the slopes of his causeways.

CHAPTER V
CRETACEOUS CRUSTACEANS

It was a cool, pleasant morning as we drove West on the Tamiami Trail. The sun was behind us and the traffic was light. Ceil and I were on the way to a Nature Conservancy Quarterly Conference in La Belle, near the Southwest shore of Lake Okeechobee. We couldn't help but be awed by the vast expance of sawgrass dotted by the numerous islands of trees. "The Everglades is like no other place on Earth," Ceil said. She had taken the very words right out of my mouth. The Miccasukee Indian Village, Forty Mile Bend and Monroe Station, in succession, reminded us each by its presence, how far along we were in our journey.

The sawgrass flats yielded to the encroaching trees until the cypress strands became the dominant scene and the grassy meadows between them became smaller and smaller. With the subtile changes in the passing scene, we realized that Ochopee and State Highway 29 weren't far. It was there that we would head North and for a half an hour or so the Fakahatchee Strand and Corkscrew Sanctuary would provide us with our next landscapes. Travelers can only see the outskirts of them as they motor along, but knowing they are there and protected from further destruction by their sanctuary status is consoling.

Deep in thought about Conservancy business coming up at the meeting in La Belle, I was startled when my wife suddenly said, "There's an oil well! They're not supposed to be here in Florida; it's too flat." We had seen many of the same kind of pumps as we drove through Texas and Oklahoma on our way to California. The hilly outskirts of Los Angeles has those great rocking arms all along the highway and even in the yards of the stores and houses. Always they had been in rolling terrain.

"The Florida ranks tenth among the United States in oil production," I answered, "and the discovery of oil in Florida dates back to the early 1940's when the state legislature offered a

$50,000 reward to the driller who brought in the first commercially feasible well."

Humble Oil and Refining Company drilled the first producing Florida well in September of 1943. They pumped over a hundred barrels per day for over thirty days to qualify for the award, added another $10,000 to it, and donated $30,000 each to the University of Florida and Florida State College for Women (now Florida State University). In addition to oil, they also pumped up a lot of water, called connate water by the oil men. In fact, they were getting about fifty-fifty oil and water. Usually the two are separated and the oil being lighter, settles to the top of the mixture. In that first Florida well, however, the oil and water were mixed together and had to separated after being pumped up to the surface. Another oddity was that the water was amazingly high in salt concentrations. So high was the salt content that they considered processing the water to obtain salt.

"The pipe for Florida's first oil well went down over two miles into the Earth," I continued, "and into a layer of limestone that was only about fifteen feet thick. What they got was an oil that was very tarry and, when processed, could only be used for fuel oil and asphalt."

"Limestone?" Ceil replied, "I thought oil formed in large pools that were trapped beneath real hard rock like granite."

I explained that that was a common misconception and that

oil was always associated with porous rocky layers underlying a non-porous layer and that both limestone and sandstone filled the bill. Since the oil forms in rock under pressure, it is squeezed and pushed around and upward through voids in the rock until it reaches an impervious layer, and there it stays. Sometimes the upper layer is dome-shaped, but not always. In the case of the Humble Oil discovery, the oil was trapped in a wedgeshaped layer of porous limestone trapped between two non-porous layers of limestone. Oil men call this stratographic entrapment.

"Another common misunderstanding is that oil is always associated with gushers," I continued.

"You mean it isn't?" Ceil asked.

"No, as a matter of fact, gushers are the exception rather than the rule. Sometimes if there is water under pressure of the surrounding rock and if the two liquids have separated, the water can act as a large piston pushing oil up from below. If the pressure is not sufficient, the driller has to pump more water down to create a greater push. This is what Humble had to do with the first Florida well. In other cases, gas may separate from the oil and be trapped above it. The trapped gas may push down on the oil from above and force it to flow up the driller's pipe. Any combination of these situations can cause a gusher, but not necessarily will there be one."

Next, my curious wife wanted to know how Humble Oil Company had ever found such a thin layer of oil-bearing limestone after drilling down more than two miles. The answer to that question was like finding the key to a mystery novel. There were many test boring sites that were used and the exact location of each was plotted on a map. As each core was brought up, it was examined closely under a microscope. The oil-bearing stratum of each was carefully noted as to its location, depth and thickness. What they discovered was apparently an old bay area of an ancient seashore. The core samples contained the fossilized remains of minute one-celled organisms called Foraminifers. Wherever oil geologists find these little critters they inspect everything more closely, because wherever they find oil, Foraminifers are close by. Upon closer microscopic inspection of the samples, they also found the fossilized remains of a unique Mesozoic clam that only lived during what geologists call the Cretaceous Period...about a hundred million years ago!

The group of clams called Rustids came into existence prior to the Cretaceous Period and had become quite common in Cretaceous seashores and bay areas. They were unique in that one of their two shells had become long and wedge-shaped, while the other had become diminuative to the extent that it only formed as a small cap over the other. The little clam animal, of course, lived inside and did all the things that clams usually do. The two shells, being calcarious or hard, would be able to keep their unique shape even under pressure and would be recognizable after all these years. Since Rustids came into existance and then disappeared completely during the Cretaceous Period, they are called an indicator group of that period and of bays that existed then.

In addition to Rustids and Foraminifers, microscopic inspection of the core samples showed the presence of calcarious or lime-producing algae. The one most commonly found was a green algal form known to thrive in shallow bays of the warm waters of the Earth. It is also known to become heavily encrusted with lime. Thus, they called it Limewort. There are still Limeworts living today and they can always be found in warm, shallow, salt or brackish waters. In close association with the green algae, the core samples from the test borings showed evidence of calcarious red and the blue-green algae. These, too, are known to inhabit the bays and estuaries today. The lime-producing capability of the three algal forms aided the oil geologists to recognize their remains, for in the absence of a limey covering, their soft tissue would have disappeared long ago.

Foraminifers, the ones that flagged the Rustids and algae, are themselves simple, one-celled, amoeba-liked members of the animal kingdom. There are living today about 18,000 different species. They are probably one of the most common and widely distributed animal groups there is. They are not only of great geographical distribution, but foraminifer's remains are among the oldest fossil remains ever to be found...going back to what Paleontologists call the Pre-Cambrian era, or some two and a half billion years! Unlike the Amoeba which thrive in fresh water, Foraminifers inhabit the seas. They have a variety of coverings that form around the one cell, but usually it is a spiny, chitinous or limey covering. Some species may attach themselves to a rock or a shell; some crawl around in the the ooze on the bottom of the sea; and there are other free-swimming species that may be found with plankton of the arctic seas as well as the tropical oceans. When the little organism dies, its calcarious covering settles to the bottom and becomes part of ooze forming in that area.

What must have happened during the early Cretaceous Period, the Humble geologists surmised from the evidence of the core samples, was that the sea level had risen gradually over a period of a few million years. The Cretaceous marine life thrived and countless generations formed layer upon layer of limey mud as they died and sank to the bay bottom. Sea worms, starfish, sea cucumbers and crustaceans of all kinds of crawled or burrowed in and over the ooze. Reef-forming Rustid species added structure to the mud. This helped keep it porous later during the cementing process as it turned into limestone. Green, blue-green and red calcareous and coralline algae acted as a jungle-like shelter for a host of fish, crabs, shrimp and other small free swimming animals. Each in their own way, for millions of years, added its mineral and protoplasm to the matrix that was to be bored and cored in 1943 by the drillers. Then it all stopped. The sea receeded (or the land was heaved up); the limey mud became exposed to atmospheric weathering and the cementing process began. In subsequent eons, the absence of Rustids that had disappeared produced a non-porous layer of limestone which trapped the oil in the lower stratum.

Paleontologists, men who study ancient rocks and life forms, think that the Cretaceous Period was one of extreme activity. There is evidence that there were a number of times when large amounts of land were submerged...as much as fifty per cent of what we see today may have been covered with sea water, and several times, apparently. By the end of that period, however, much of North America was as we know it today. Fossil evidence shows that land plants which existed were also very similar to those surrounding us now. Apparently, there were great forests of evergreen and deciduous trees in the temperate zones of the Earth; palm trees, ferns and horse tails inhabited the tropical regions. Evidence seems to point to the fact that the plains type ecosystems would develop in subsequent eras, but there were, however, great areas of fresh water wetlands as well as vast brackish savannahs.

During the latter part of the Cretaceous Period, dinosaurs were at the height of their development. They were by far the dominant land animals, but they were soon to lose their unchallenged status. Few fossil remains of mammals have been uncovered in the Cretaceous strata of rock. Fossils that have been uncovered are those of small secretive, furry animals like shrews and moles. They were plant eaters and insectivores. Fossil remains of pouch-bearing animals similar to the oppossum have also been found. As might be expected, because of the increase in insectivore mammals, insects and spiders were becoming numerous in both numbers and species. It seems evident from the fossil evidence found worldwide, that by the end of the Cretaceous Period, air, land and sea flora and fauna were very much as we know them today with a few exceptions.

It is difficult to determine exactly how often sea level rose and fell, but each layer of limestone in the core samples is mute evidence that it did. There may have been several glacial and inter-glacial periods and there were times when the land warped up and downward. That Florida has been below and above sea level is not doubted by anyone who has seen the evidence. Each time our State underwent one of these stratigraphic changes, the Cretaceous Crustacians and their associated marine forms were buried deeper and deeper under successively new layers of limestone. As pressure increased, heat was produced. Under the influence of both and in the absence of air, animal and plant protoplasm decayed away, but the fatty and oily tissues were slowly converted by a physio-chemical process to what we now call petroleum.

"There are Sandy and June!" Ceil said as we pulled into La Belle. We had all been told in our Nature Conservancy Bulletin to meet at the West side of the town square. From there we would follow the leader out to Jessie's place where a field trip and business meeting were to be held. Ceil, Sandy and June decided to stretch their legs while we waited for the rest of the gang to show up. I could hear my wife as they walked away. She was saying, "Do you realize that as we all drove to La Belle we were performing the curtain call for a fascinating drama the scenes of which have been enacted for hundreds of millions of years involving a cast of billions of generations of actors?"

GLOSSARY FOR CHAPTER V

1. Amoeba—minute, one-celled protozoa. (See also protozoa in the Glossary for Chapter III.)
2. Calcareous Structure—see Glossary for Chapter IV.
3. Calcareous Algae—even though algae are members of the Plant Kingdom, certain marine species are capable of secreting a limey encrustation on their outer surface. They are referred to as calcareous algae or limeworts.
4. Chitinous—Covering—a fairly hard outer protective covering produced by many lower forms of animal life such as insects and crustaceans.
5. Connate Water—water that is mixed with petroleum as the two are pumped out of the ground together from the earth. Sometimes the two are separated from each other as the petroleum is discovered and it can just be pumped from above the surface of the water. In the case of most oil found in Florida, the two are mixed and must be separated after they are recovered. Usually water that is so closely mixed with the oil, as in the case of the Florida product, is extremely salty.
6. Cretaceous Period—a geological era that dates way back to the latter portion of the Age of Dinosaurs or about sixty to seventy million years ago.
7. Crustaceans—a group of animals that has a chitinous outer covering, or exoskeleton. The group includes such animals as crabs, lobsters, and barnacles.
8. Cypress Strand—The big cypress swamp near the western edge of the Everglades is a relatively flat tropical prairie. Any slight depression will collect water and provide a natural growing area for cypress trees. If the depressed area is greatly elongated, the resulting strip of cypress trees is called a strand.
9. Ecosystem—see Glossary for Chapter II.
10. Fauna—see Glossary for Chapter I.

11. Flora—see Glossary for Chapter I.
12. Foraminifer—see Glossary for Chapter III.
13. Granite—a basement rock for the earth. It is derived from the fluid-like magma deep below the earth's surface.
14. Insectivore—an animal (some authors also include plants) which feeds on insects as its only, or at least main, source of food.
15. Limestone—see Glossary for Chapter II.
16. Limewort—see Calcareous Algae in this Glossary.
17. Mesozoic Era—a geological period of time that began some 180 million years ago and is otherwise known as The Age of Reptiles.
18. Miccasukee Indians—(there are a variety of ways to spell the name) a tribe of Indians that broke away from the Seminoles at the conclusion of the Florida War (see Glossary for Chapter I). Their present tribal reservation is about forty miles west of Miami.
19. Paleontologist—a scientist who studies the fossil remains of plants and animals.
20. Plankton—a collective term which includes a myriad of microscopic and plants and animals, living on or near the surface of the ocean.
21. Pre-Cambrian Era—a geological period referring to a time over two-and-a-half billion years ago, when only minute, simple forms of life existed.
22. Protoplasm—the soft, living portion of the cells of both fauna and flora.
23. Rustids—an extinct form of clam (or shellfish) that existed during the Cretaceous Period. Like clams, rustids have two shells that are hinged together; unlike clams, the two shells of rustids are not the mirror image of each other. Instead, one of the shells is greatly elongated and cone-shaped, while the other is a simple small circular cap that fits over its cone-shaped counterpart.
24. Sandstone—a sedimentary form of rock, formed from a sandy sediment.
25. Savannah—a flat, treeless grassland. In Florida most savannahs are flooded at least a good portion of the time with brackish water.
26. Stratographic Change—a change that has been brought

about by natural forces acting on the strata of rock in an area. The change could involve either the addition of new layers or the shifting of layers of rock with respect to each other, and so forth.
27. Stratographic Entrapment—used in this story, Stratographic entrapment of oil has occurred when the porous layer of limestone which contained oil was wedged between two non-porous layers so that the oil was trapped in place.

CHAPTER VI
FROM THE DEVIL'S MILL HOPPER DOWN

The headlines read "Sinkhole Develops Quickly!" The story that followed elaborated that "Two workers, scrambling for their lives, barely made it to safety before the well drilling rig they were on disappeared into a sinkhole..." In less than a minute the hole became about thirty four feet in diameter and some fifty feet deep and gulped into its gullet a quarter of a million dollar drilling rig, a truck loaded with drilling pipes, and a large quantity of expensive drilling tools. Even more significant, however, the funnelshaped hole swallowed the drillers' anchor to reality. As I read the article in the paper, I tried to imagine what it must have felt like to those two men. One minute they were standing on good old solid Earth-all their lives they had put their feet down and there it was just as dependable and predictable as the ebb and flow of the tides-next minute they had to scratch and claw for their lives as Mother Earth pursed her lips and tried to suck them into her maw.

Later, Fred spoke to me about the experience. He said that they were drilling at about 400 feet when they lost circulation. Within seconds a slight depression began to form and all they could think of was getting out of there. The ground seemed to sink away behind them as they ran; it was like running uphill but the land was flat. I asked him what it means to "...lose circulation" and he told me it was a drillers' term. When they drill deep wells they circulate water down with the rotary drill head to help keep it cool and to circulate the cuttings away. As the water circulates back up to the surface, the cuttings are removed and the water is reused. Lost circulation, then, refers to loss of the returning water with the cuttings. When this happens, it means they have hit an underground cavern and water is pouring into it.

"It's the same principle as taking a garden hose and placing the nozzle against the ground. When you turn the water on, the stream will wash the soil away and you can just keep poking the hose down in the hole you create", Fred said. "If you poked your hose through the ceiling of a cave, there'd be no back pressure and the water would try to fill the cave up." That's exactly what happened to Fred and his fellow worker. Sometimes when they hit a strong underground stream they will get more "return water" than they are pumping down into the hole. Either way, however, they are a little leery because of the possibility of cave-ins. Now, Fred admitted, he will be even more apprehensive in the future when he loses circulation.

Sinkholes, of course, are not a new phenomenon to anybody who has lived in Florida very long. Probably the most renowned sink is the one that was reported in May, 1981 in the Winter

Park area (near Orlando). It was a little over one thousand feet in diameter and about 170 feet deep. As this huge plug of ground settled down to fill the void beneath, it took part of a major highway and several businesses with it. Then when it filled up with water everything was lost forever. During the decade of the Sixties, seventy-one sinkholes formed near Tampa, Florida. Twenty of them formed in one really dry winter. Not all sinks fill with water, though. Where the ground water is at a lower elevation than the bottom of the sink hole, it can be just a dry depression in the ground. On the other hand, if a sink forms near a pourous layer of limestone that is saturated with water, it can fill up quite rapidly and in this latter case, the sink will form an almost circular lake.

My first introduction to the phenomenon of sinks was when I was a student at the University fo Florida. Just a few miles North and West of Gainesville is a place called "The Devil's Mill Hopper". It was nearly as great in diameter as a football field is long. The steep, sloping sides were overgrown with huge trees and an understory of smaller trees and shrubs. There were numerous little trails spiralling downward around the sides where many feet had worn them into the bank. I'll never forget the first time I stood on the brink of the hopper and looked down on the tops of those great oaks. It was in the fall and bright-colored leaves were everywhere. In my youthful exuberance I started down the slope and soon learned that the paths were to be supplemented by holding on to anything I could grab hold of from vines and extruding roots to branches and the trunks of sapling trees.

After I had slipped and slid about fifteen to twenty feet I noticed that water was oozing out of the ground almost as if it were a tiny spring. There was a small, damp area where the exuding water had eroded the soil to form a flat muddy area, and strewn all around were small pebbles and other material. I let my feet slidedown until I was sitting beside the spring for a closer look. I spotted a small sharks tooth among the pebbles. Soon I was scratching in the mud for more of them. Noting where the place was so I could return, I decided to continue on my downward trip to see what other wonderous things this marvelous hole in the ground had in store for me. There were more springs, of course; the underbrush got thicker; the trees got a little smaller; plants began to look strange; and the paths became fewer but more distinct. Finally, down near the bottom there was an amazing collection of swampy plants, sand mixed with mud, boulders, branches, and old decaying logs. It never dawned on me on the way down that water, dirt, rocks, and dead trees had no other place to go when gravity took hold of them.

Here at the lowest level my other senses were perceiving another sensation that I hadn't fully become conscious of. Hot from exertion of my downward trip, I soon realized it was darker, cooler, and damper than it was at the top. I was later to discover on a class field trip that some of the flora near the bottom of The Devil's Mill Hopper were, indeed, unique in Florida. They undergo shorter and cooler days in both summer and winter and, for that reason, some are more typical of the flora of the Piedmont in the Carolinas. This was specially true of the ferns.

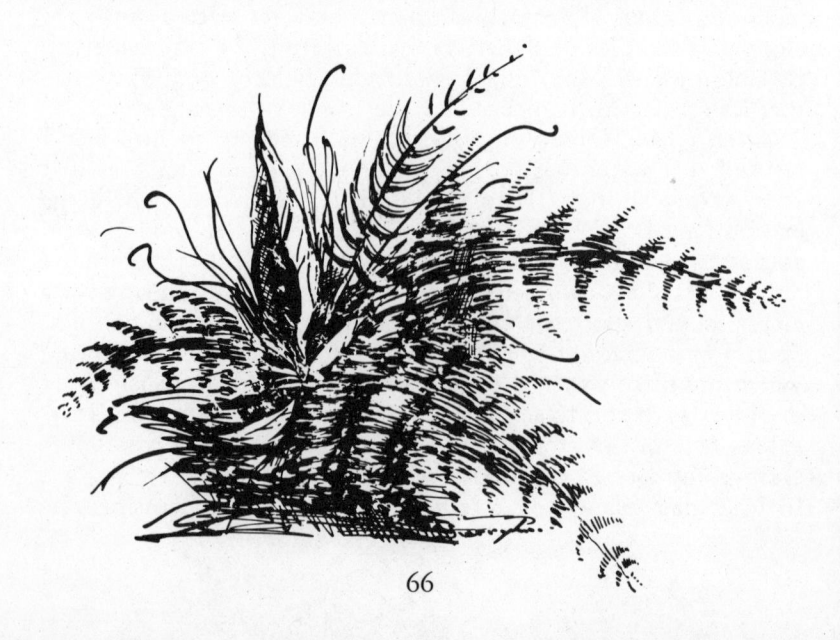

All the way down I had been wondering where the water went. Now I found myself at the place where the numerous trickling springs coverged to form a small marsh. The rivulettes that flowed down the sides of the hopper were not able to fill it up with water and I set myself to the task of finding out why. Soon I found the answer. Off to one side of the marshy bottom and below the steepest slope was a small cave. Into it the water flowed in a steady stream and, getting close, I could hear the trickle but the hole was too small to see what was happening or where the water was going. In my youthful mind, I imagined the water trying to follow Jules Verne into the very bowels of the Earth.

If The Devil's Mill Hopper had had a larger cave at its lowest point, I probably would have crawled into it to follow that stream as far as I possibly could. There are many caves in the Gainesville area that are explorable, though, and "Speelunking" in them is quite popular now. It also gives the explorer some real insight as to how caves and caverns are formed. Once you realize that limestone is soluble in acid, and add to that knowledge the fact that decaying vegetation produces organic acid which the rain water picks up as it percolates down through the soil, you have the main ingredients for cave and cavern formation in pourous limestone.

The downward movement of rainwater through the soil causes it to become more and more acidic until finally it reaches the underlying limestone. "Soaking" into the porous stone, it continues its downward movement dissolving the limestone as it goes until it reaches an impervious layer. At that point the water "flows" downhill along the upper surface of the "confining layer", as it is called. The downward and lateral movement of acidic water through the porous limestone produces a sort of internal erosion. Given thousands, even millions of years, the cracks and fissures become larger and larger until a complex network of interconnecting caverns and caves is created.

There are instances where scuba divers have entered a cave at the bottom of a sink hole filled with water, followed a maze of tunnels and caverns, and emerged from another sink more than a mile away. Sometimes, along the way, they may reach a cave that has air trapped in it and can remove their gear to rest a moment. Studying the ceilings and floors of underground caves reveals water dripping from above where it seeps down through the limestone. If it hesitates a while some of the dissolved limestone may percipitate out leaving a little deposit on the ceiling. As this material builds up over the years, the deposited calcareous substance creates what geologists call a stalactite. If the bottom of the cave is dry, the water dripping off a stalactite can still contain enough dissolved material to create a mirror image of itself on the floor.

Given time, the stalactite and its companion stalagmite can even connect to each other and produce an hourglass-shaped column. It is easily understood, then, how a system of tunels, caverns, and caves connecting each other both horizontally and vertically can become so extensive that water is able to flow back and forth quite freely and for considerable distances. Studies have shown that water can flow from lakes into a nearby cavern network when the water level in the lake is higher than the pressure level of the water in the caverns. The reverse is true as well.

The interesting thing about all this is that Peninsular Florida is underlain by a huge layer of limestone which varies in thickness from about 1500 feet to 2500 feet thick. It is called the Floridan Aquifer. Since it slopes gently to the Southeast its upper limits start at about 300 feet below the surface near the central highlands of Florida but are some 900 to 1000 feet below the surface in the Miami area. A Geologists definition of the Floridan Aquifer would sound something like this: it is a complex set of limestone layers, or aquifers, that were formed between the middle Eocene and the middle Miocene, or from about one hundred million years ago to about five million years ago.

That complex system of aquifers called the Floridan implies that over all those millions of years that it was being formed, many different layers were deposited-each with its own set of characteristics and properties. Some are very porous and others absorb very little water. In general, however, there are two primary layers. The upper-most is the artesian layer and is where fresh water is obtained for most commercial wells; the lower layer-the boulder zone-is much more cavernous and filled with salt water. It was probably the upper limits of the boulder zone where Fred lost circulation with his drilling rig. When he hit the ceiling of a large cavern with his drill he probably broke the delicate balance of forces which supported it and a whole plug of Earth 45 feet wide and 350 feet long dropped down into the void.

Most of the water in the tunnels of the artesian zone of the Floridan Aquifer is replenished by rainwater which falls on the highlands area round Lake, Polk, and Highlands Counties. When the water reaches a confining layer of limestone, it will "flow" slowly toward the Atlantic Ocean to the East or to the Gulf of Mexico to the West. When it reaches a point where the limestone out-crops beneath the salty seas, it will "seep" out into the sea in the form of an underwater, fresh water spring. This probably occurs at several hundred feet below sea level and five to 10 miles out to sea. There is empirical evidence to support to the idea, that sea water actually "flows" into the Floridan Aquifer at the greater depths in the boulder zone. It enters the aquifer farther out to sea than the fresh water springs occur.

Geologists know, for instance, that the temperature increases as they drill deeper and deeper. Temperature checks have been made in test wells that have been drilled as much as 12 to 15,000 feet below sea level. Near the Axis of Florida this geothermal energy warms water in the caverns of the boulder zone. The water then rises by convection to a point near the upper limit of that zone. The rising water then circulates Eastward and Westward toward the ocean and the Gulf and eventually manifests itself as deep salt water springs emerging from the sea bottom far away from the Florida Peninsula.

Sometimes the sea water makes its way to the surface of the Earth through the network of underground caverns and tunnels and arrives at ground level by the way of an old sink hole. It then flows out of the bowels of the Earth in the form of a hot mineral spring. Located in Southwest Florida there are spas that act as mute evidence of what is occurring deep into the ground below Florida. There is speculation that very little interaction occurs between the upper artesian zone of the Floridan Aquifer and the lower saline boulder zone. The numerous layers of limestone are thought to have at least one fairly well-defined, impervious layer separating the two primary zones. The presence of mineral springs, however, seems to dispel the notion.

The ingenuity of man is never to be doubted...questioned, maybe, but not doubted. With the knowledge gained concerning the Floridan Aquifer and its circulation of fresh water at the upper level, we have learned to tap a source of precious fresh water for muncipal consumption, industrial uses, and agricultural irrigation. It seems as though it is an inexhaustible supply of water. After all it is only a few hundred feet thick but it underlies most of Peninsular Florida. Plans have even been carried through to inject fresh water into the artesian zone during the rainy season when water is plentiful and then recall that water during the dry season—a nature-built underground storage tank, so to speak. The process in theory, is merely speeding up the recharging process that mother nature does with rain and it assures that the aquifer will be recharged to its maximum capacity. With an ever increasing population, Florida needs some sort of assurance that water will be available all year round.

The idea of deep well injection into the aquifer has even been carried out one step further. Many such wells have been sunk for the purpose of waste disposal into the boulder zone. Sewage water, industrial waste, brine from desalination plants of oil wells have all been pumped down some 3,000 feet into the boulder zone of the Floridan Aquifer in hopes that it will rise with the circulating sea water and "flow" out to the Atlantic Ocean or the Gulf. Mixing of the drinking water and the waste water is highly unlikely, the proponents say, because the wells are drilled far apart from each other and the two layers of the aquifer are separated by an impervious layer of limestone. There are twenty, thirty, even more of these deep injection wells. They have been in existance for more than twenty years and are carefully monitored.

Sinkholes, like the one that almost swallowed Fred, are only a small part of the whole story. They represent the first link of a chain of voids that leads downward and outward in all directions. One can get lost in a maze, however, and, bumping into several deadends, never find their way out. Maybe my youthful musing about where the water flows from The Devil's Mill Hopper was more prophetic than I realized.

GLOSSARY FOR CHAPTER VI

1. Artesian Zone—the zone of the Floridan Aquifer from which most communities in peninsular Florida obtain their drinking water. Also most commercial water wells tap this source and most agricultural water comes from it, as well.
2. Aquifer—a layer of porous limestone from which potable water can be obtained.
3. Axis of Florida—an imaginary line that would bisect the peninsula of Florida half way between the Continental Shelf in the Atlantic Ocean and the continental Shelf in the Gulf of Mexico.
4. Boulder Zone—the deepest portion of the Floridan Aquifer. It is characterized by having numerous caves and caverns which means that it is highly porous. Because of the great porosity and because it out-crops from both the Atlantic Ocean and the Gulf of Mexico, it is filled with salty water.
5. Calcareous Structure—see Glossary for Chapter IV.
6. Confining Layer—a non-porous layer of limestone, either above or below a porous layer which restricts the transmission of fluid from the porous layer to an adjacent one.
7. Cuttings—well-drillers force water down around the drill head for the purpose of cooling the drill bit and flushing the rock particles away as they dig. The water pumped downward for this purpose usually circulates back to the surface, flushing rock and other debris up with it. The rock and debris that are raised to the surface are called "cuttings." When the drillers "lose circulation," it is an indication that they have penetrated into an underground cavern; the water with its cuttings, no longer returns to the surface, but instead starts to fill up the cavern.
8. Deep-Well Injection—the reverse process of pumping water from a well. In deep-well injection, water and waste fluids are forced, under high pressure, into porous limestone, usually the boulder zone where waste water is concerned

and usually into the artesian zone where potable water is involved.

9. Eocene Epoch—a geological period of time that began about fifty million years ago and ended about forty million years ago.
10. Flora—see Glossary for Chapter I.
11. Floridan Aquifer—this aquifer is well described in the story, however, it underlies all of peninsular Florida and is from 1,500 to 2,500 feet thick depending upon where the measurements are taken. The "Floridan" is generally thought to be a complex system of lesser aquifers—some being more porous that others. It is divided into two major levels, called zones that are referred to as the artesian zone and the boulder zone which are described at some length under their own name in this glossary.
12. Geothermal Energy—it is well known by those who drill deep holes in the earth that the deeper they drill the higher the temperature becomes. The heat energy produced by natural forces deep inside the earth is referred to as geothermal energy.
13. Highlands of Florida—lie slightly East of the Axis of Florida. (See Axis of Florida in this Glossary.) Roughly, the highlands' central area is near Lakeland; they extend fifty or so miles, north and south.
14. Hot Springs—occur when underground water from deep inside the earth rises to the surface through a series of interconnected caverns and fissures. The water, heated by geothermal energy, rises by convection; it is generally very salty.
15. Limestone—see Glossary for Chapter II.
16. Lost Circulation—See "Cuttings" in this Glossary.
17. Miocene—See Glossary for Chapter III.
18. Percolate—see Glossary for Chapter II.
19. Piedmont—the foothills along the Southern edge of the Appalachian Mountains are referred to as the Piedmont area or section.
20. Precipitate—See Stalactite in this Glossary.
21. Recharge of an Aquifer—as fresh water either circulates away or is pumped away form an area in an aquifer, its replacement in the form of ground water rain or from main

or nearby lakes or rivers is called recharging the aquifer. Ultimately, of course, all recharging of aquifers is from the rain.

22. Scuba—an acronym for Self-Contained Underwaer Breathing Apparatus. Underwater divers wear the apparatus so they can remain submerged for extended periods of time.
23. Sinkhole—refers to a large depression in the surface of the earth, assumed to have been caused by the collapse of large underground caverns that lay directly below where the sink is located. Some of them fill up with nearby ground water and some are not filled with water.
24. Speelunking—the sport of exploring underground caverns that have filled with water; the explorers use scuba apparatus so they can breath under water. Sometimes air is trapped in the cavern above the water level and the scuba gear can be removed. (See Scuba in this Glossary.)
25. Stalactites—deposits of pure limestone (calcite) that are suspended from the ceilings of limestone caves and caverns. The stalactites remind one of icicles hanging from the eaves of a roof. As water percolates downward through the limestone above the cavern, it accumulates more and more dissolved calcite until sometimes there is an over abundance of calcite dissolved in the water. As this "super-saturated" water collects on the roof of the cavern and hesitates before it drips, some of the calcite crystallizes out of solution and is left behind by the drop. (Chemists called this process precipitation.) Another way stalactites form is by evaporation. If the downward percolation of water is so slow that a drop on the ceiling of a cavern evaporates before the next drop arrives, all the calcite that was dissolved in it is left behind. As the solution dries up the calcite crystallizes out as in the first situation.
26. Stalagmites—look like icicles, "growing" up from the floors of limestone caverns. They generally, are right below a stalactite and are formed in the same identical way. In some cases, if the stalactite "grows" down far enough to to meet its companion stalagmite, the two will merge to form a column. (See Stalactite in this Glossary.)

CHAPTER VII
KISSIMMEE RIVER REVISITED

As we drifted lazily with the current, Pete cast his Dalton Special (it has to have the frog finish, according to him) in all the nooks and coves he could find. It was a top water lure and he wasn't getting as many strikes as I was, but that didn't make any difference. Once he remarked that there was no greater thrill to him than having a large-mouth bass strike a top water plug. "There's that faint ripple in the water, then just before the strike you see the water mound up almost like a submarine just surfacing. Almost simultaneously the water opens up, flies everywhere at once, and with a silvery flash it all closes right back. It's almost as though the water itself is devouring your plug," he said. "Then you have to be sure to set the hook before old Mr. Bass spits it out. Sometimes I got so excited I'd jerk it right out of his mouth before he's hooked. There's just nothing like it!"

We were at our favorite spot just south of Lake Kissimmee fishing the west bank of the Kissimmee River. Right after the rainy season the water is fairly high. Sometimes it overflows its banks and floods the adjacent pasture lands. At flood stage, there is an almost imperceptible current that moves you along just a little more slowly than one of those low horsepower electric motors, I took the paddle in my hand and eased it into the water to assure that we drifted a good casting distance from the button bushes, maidencane and arrowhead plants which told us where the water was shallow. "I read somewhere," I said softly, "that a raindrop would take over a year to flow from the North end of the Upper Kissimmee Basin through the chain of lakes, the Kissimmee River, Lake Okeechobee and on through the Everglades to finally reach the Bay of Florida and the Gulf of Mexico."

"Uh-Uh," Pete replied as though he were really saying "Be quiet! You'll scare the fish!" When he fishes, everything else fades into oblivion. I've figured out that Pete usually catches more fish than I do because he's so intense about it and I have a tendency to let my mind wander.

As I was manuvering our boat for him to cast, I couldn't help but reflect on this wonderous water system nature has fashioned. In the year's time it would take that hypothetical drop of water to reach the sea, there are several interesting possibilities that could happen to it. The source of all water in the system is rain and three-fourths of it showers down between May and October. Not all of the little drops get to flow to the sea, however. over ninety per cent of them evaporate back into the atmosphere only to fall again later as rain or condense out as dew in the cool mornings. The ten per cent that remains is what we see as river, lake marsh, and swamp. Some of it soaks into the ground to help raise the water table or to recharge an aquifer.

"What takes it so long?" Pete burst into my thoughts like a bass hitting his top-water plug.

"What takes what so long?" I responded somewhat surprised.

"The raindrop you were talking about."

"Well, first it has to make its way through a chain of lakes and where the volume is great, the rate of flow is very slow. When it reaches the river, the route is circuitous, for the Kissimmee River twists and braids its way 130 miles to travel only slightly more than fifty miles as the crow flies. In an exceptionally hard rainstorm when the river overflows, the water is slowed further by spikerush, spatterdock, smart weed, and other marshy plants that grow in the flood plain." Then I continued to explain that the story repeats itself again as water reaches Lake Okeechobee and, finally, the Everglades. The 'Glades' are so flat and sawgrass so thick that a drop may not flow more than a few feet in twenty-four hours.

"Uh-Uh," was Pete's response to all that. He was concentrating on movement in the grass just behind his plug.

Sometimes I think Pete just asks those leading questions to keep me talking. That way I don't fish as much nor do I mind my business when I do fish, and that's why he catches more than I do. With determination I threw my Johnson Spoon at a likely looking spot. It quickly sank out of sight in the dark water and I began my jerky retrieve. Fishing is usually slower when the water is high because the fish can spread out; they have more places to go. They leave the main run of the river and seek the flooded marshy overflow with its numerous intermittent ponds. Then later in the season, when the ponds begin to dry up, the fish become a concentrated source of nourishment for the aquatic birds.

"The swamps and marshy wetlands are the river's Kidney's," an old timer at the fish camp once told me. They slow down the flow so that particles suspended in the water can settle out. The miriad plants utilize nitrate and phosphate chemicals as nourishment. Water soaking into the soil and then seeping back out at a lower level is filtered in the process and, hence, is purified, clean water. The cleansed ground water deep below the surface is what we tap when we drill our shallow wells to get our water. Deeper still, water will pass from the overburden of soil into the pourous limestone base. Here it can remain stored for years at a time and can become available for deep wells drilled at great distances from the river.

Absorption of water by the Earth is a storage mechanism that carries plants and animals through the seven or so months when rain is scarce. The plants have adapted to the feast and famine cycle. The tops die back in the winter months and little or no water is needed when it is scarce in the soil. With the coming of the Spring rains, however, seeds germinate and old root stocks sprout with new growth. The annual plants mature quickly with the lengthening of day so that flowers and their inevitable product, the seed, soon abound. The larger trees and bushes, of course, have a root system which can still tap the lowering water table in the dry months. They, too, have adapted to the hydrologic cycle and require much less ground water in the dry season. Many lose their leaves and others grow very little when days are short.

The animals have adapted as well. Fish make their nest and spawn when the water is high and there is plenty of food and cover. Birds nest and have young at the time when ponds are drying up and the fish and frogs are concentrated in low, deep water holes. Then, with advent of spring rains, the river deepens, water holes re-connect and the fish fan out to spawn again. Over the thousands of years, the annual rise and fall of the water has followed rainy season and drought. Both plants and animals have reached an equilibrium in which the strongest and most adaptive have survived.

"There he is!" Pete exclaimed. A lunker had grabbed his lure and was shaking it like a bulldog tugging on a knotted sock.

"He's a beauty," said Pete as the bass broke through the surface. "I'll bet he'll go seven pounds!"

"Don't let him tangle up your line," I replied. "Hold your rod up," I said and then I laughed out loud at myself. Pete taught me how to fish. I hadn't fished with anything but a cane pole till I came out to the river with him. Pete's bass was finally in the boat and with sunset tinting the Western sky a brilliant orange, we decided to call it day.

"Let's go back to our old favorite spot on the Kissimmee river." The words were spoken somewhat in jest and with a note of sadness, too. Thirty years had passed since Pete caught that last bass. We had both gone our separate ways to make a living and raise our families. Ceil and I had left town and then returned to spend the rest of our days "back home." Pete had fallen in with some friends who loved salt water fishing and, although he remained right here, had seldom ventured West to the river.

"It isn't the same anymore." he replied.

"I know," I said, "the Corps of Engineers has channelized the river. They don't even call it a river anymore." What was once the beautiful, pristine Kissimmee River now bears the impersonal, degrading title of C-38. In the short span of time that had passed, "progress" along the Western edge of the Kissimmee River wetland system had turned it from cypress domes and strands bordered by pineland and hardwood systems into farmland, improved pasture, and residential development. Pasture lands that comprised some eight per cent to ten per cent in 1953 now occupy forty per cent to fifty per cent of the Lower Kissimmee Basin. Concomitantly, wetlands have been reduced from well over fifty per cent of the basin's total area to less than a quarter of it's area. The sad thing about it is that this seems to be the pattern throughout the United States. The U.S. Fish and Wildlife Service has estimated a loss of almost half a million acres of wetlands per year for the past quarter of a century...and well over threefourths of all that has occurred in the Southeastern States.

"I was talking to Grady just the other day about how serious the loss of wetlands is," I continued. As if to illustrate what has been happening, he said his father used to carry mail in the late 1800's. He picked it up once a week in Eau Gallie and carried it by horseback West to Fort Christmas. From there he went to St. Cloud, Holopaw, Kennansville and Fort Drum. Then he crossed over to the East Coast and went back North to Eau Gallie.

Grady said his father told him that often, during the rainy season the St. Johns River flood plain and the North end of the Kissimmee River System merged and that after he and his horse swam the St. Johns River they would be wading in water all the way to Fort Christmas!

"That's hard to believe in 1985," said Pete. "Cities and towns up and down Florida's East Coast are feuding over water now because it's so scarce."

We mulled that one over for a while and then began to discuss related problems brought on by the channelization of the Kissimmee River. The Corps' main purpose for the project was flood control. In order to accomplish that purpose, they constructed six structures between the South end of Lake Kissimmee and the Northern shore of Lake Okeechobee. Since the difference in elevation of the two lakes is about thirty feet, each structure, or lock, lowers the water level about five feet. Thus, during the rainy season there are six waterfalls and five canals connecting the two lakes. In dry season there are two natural lakes and five artificial lakes that are each thirty feet deep, fifty feet wide, and ten miles long. Of course, flood prevention has been achieved and with locks included in the structures, the "river" is navigable even during dry season.

One of the greatest side effects created by the flood control is the transfer of tens of thousands of acres of wetlands from wet prairie, marsh, swamp and braided river to improved pasture and other agricultural land. This might not be perceived as a problem if you were an upland property owner. Now your property would be well drained and more valuable. It's so valuable, in fact, that you're fighting tooth and claw to prevent returning the river to its original state. Several plans have been proposed not the least of which involves removing the structures and backfilling C-38. There are various other lesser options. All the proposals involve "buying back," at taxpayers expense, the land that was once wetland so that some of it can become wetland again!

The Kissimmee River Basin used to discharge water into the lake gradually over a long period of time. Now the rapid, straight flow of water into Lake Okeechobee has caused both water conservation and water quality problems. Water flows into the lake three times as fast as it did in pre-C-38 days. The rapid flow of the canal and its inability to overflow its banks means rain falling in the valley upstream will not only reach the lake faster, but it will not soak into the soil. This was the whole idea—flood control. At the same time, however, soil water is diminished and the recharging of the various aquifers is not so great. Water quality suffers along with the rapid run-off because it is no longer filtered. Lateral canals which drain the upland pastures and agricultural lands carry water filled with animal waste, insecticides, and fertilizer chemicals. These impurities are more abundant at the very time when natural filtering is not occurring.

The combination of faster river flow and increased impurities during the rainy season has created problems with lake level management. Water gets to the lake from all upstream sources sooner in the season...and there is more of it. Rising lake levels when they rise too high or too fast mean that the lake must be lowered by discharging excess water East through the St. Lucie Canal, Southwesterly through the Caloosahatchee River, or Southeasterly through a network of canals to the water conservation areas of Broward and Dade Counties. Water thus released from the system cannot be conserved within the system. Illustrative of loss of quality is the fact that there have been more algae blooms and fish-kills in the Northern end of lake Okeechobee than there ever were before C-38 was completed. Many believe that this has been caused by unfiltered contaminants overstimulating aquatic plants growing there. This robs the lake water of its dissolved oxygen. Once the process begins and fish start suffocating and dying it is a self-feeding mechanism. Decay of the dead and dying aquatic animals and plants uses up even more of the precious oxygen....which kills even more fish.

Yet another problem associated with channelization of the Kissimmee River is the effect it has had on the native flora and fauna of the valley. In the pre-channelization days the flood plain and the valley beyond supported year-round residents such as Florida duck, coot, egrets and other aquatic birds, water rat, raccoon, deer, turkey, aligators, bass and a wide assortment of pan fish. It also served as winter quarters for a large assortment of migratory birds. With loss of habitat-i.e., the braided river and its associated marshes and wet prairies-there has been a sharp reduction in both resident and migratory fauna.

"What do you mean by 'loss of habitat?'" Pete asked. "The land is still there and it hasn't been developed."

"Even though the land hasn't been paved over and covered with shopping centers and houses," I said, "it's still been developed. Improved pasture is development; lateral drainage canals are development; the spoil banks of the various canals are development. By loss of wildlife habitat, I mean the plant eating animals have lost the leaves, flowers, and seeds that they feed on with each change in the season. Then when they disappear the predators leave, as well. Some of the native plants grow rapidly in the spring and their flowers turn to seed, then they rest. While they rest, another group blooms in the summer; as they then rest, yet another group of plants bloom in the Fall. This continues throughout each season with those that mature in the fall providing mast throughout the coming dry season. Plant-eating animals depend on this variety of diet for survival. Where there was once a wide variety of grasses and other annual prairie and marsh plants there is now pasture, dog fennel, and wax myrtle that weren't so common before."

The Corps of Engineers has recognized the succession of plant species brought on by the loss of flooding and, with it, the diminishing variety of wildlife. In order to combat the side effect to flood control, they have tried "manipulating" the water levels of the lower two sections of C-38. By "manipulating" they mean raising the elevation of the structure in order to make the channel spill over its banks and flood surrounding terrain. There has been a minimal return to "normal conditions" near the South end of each of these last two sections. That is to say, there is still a nine mile long, fifty foot wide body of water with a sort of triangular-shaped marshy area covering the last mile or so and terminating with a dam and lock. The marsh near the south end is similar to the original habitat that existed prior to channelization, but by no means as extensive.

"Aren't there people who are trying to get the Kissimmee River restored to its original state?" Pete asked. The answer to this is not quite so simple as it sounds. By "restore," is meant restore as much as possible but still maintain acceptable levels of flood control. The bottom line is that the river will *never* again be the way it was at the turn of the century. Several plans for "restoration" have been proposed.

The most costly calls for backfilling parts of the channel and opening up parts of the old river bed along with removing some of the existing structures and replacing them with a system of gated culverts and weirs and low lateral levees. There would be "pool manipulation" upstream from remaining structures. This plan would allow water to flow through about two thirds of the original river while still retaining almost half of the existing canal. It is estimated that this plan would ultimately increase wetland acreage as much as 7000 acres. It might also decrease the amount of existing wetlands and it is the most costly plan. At an estimated $82 million with possible further loss of wetlands it seems like the least desireable option.

Probably the least costly "restoration" plan, according to the Corps of Engineers is what they call the "Pool Stage Manipulation Plan." Simply put the plan calls for raising the elevation of each existing structure about two feet so that the wetlands could be flooded near the end of the rainy season. Then beginning in November the impounded water would be released slowly to about one foot below their present levels to simulate low water conditions during the original dry season. Associated with this plan would be the need for longer and higher lateral dikes at each structure to prevent water from "flowing around" during the high water stage of the synthetic cycle. The manipulation plan is estimated to cost about six million dollars initially, but it would require about half a million dollars annually to maintain. It would restore about one forth of the original wetlands that have been lost.

The third major plan being considered is referred to as the "Combined Wetlands Plan." The plan incorporates manipulation of water levels of the pools upstream from the existing structures as outlined in the Pool Stage Manipulation Plan. In addition, by building a complex network of lateral levees with weirs and gated culverts, there would be several "flow-through" marshes and tributary impoundments. There would also be several areas where water would flow through the old river bed as well as through C-38. With it all, the Corps of Engineers would try to recreate almost half of the original wetlands during high water season at a cost of almost thirty three million dollars, plus 2.7 million dollars annually thereafter for maintenance and operation.

By this time in our discussion Pete was completely overwhelmed with the situation. He said, "Why did you suggest that we go back to fish our favorite hot spot? It isn't even there any more. If we were out there right now and if the old fishing hole were still there at least I could be concentrating on catching that bass instead of listening to all your chatter. It's too bad that we'll never see it again even if they do 'restore' it."

GLOSSARY FOR CHAPTER VII

1. Aquifer—see Glossary for Chapter VI.
2. Fauna—see Glossary for Chapter I.
3. Flora—see Glossary for Chapter I.
4. Ft. Christmas—located near where the modern town of Christmas, Florida is now situated. It was, roughly North and West of Eau Gallie (now part of Melbourne) and about half way to Orlando.
5. Hydrologic Cycle—the cyclical occurrence of water available to the plants of an area. In the portions of Florida that surrounded the Kissimmee River the rainy season is from May to September of each year and there is usually plenty of water available for both flora and fauna. Beginning around October the rain is not so frequent nor is it as heavy. Less that twenty per cent of the annual rainfall occurs between October and April. Then in May the cycle begins a new.
6. Limestone—see Glossary for Chapter II.

CHAPTER VIII
A LOST CAUSE

We had been hunting since we arrived at camp about noon that day. A cold front had moved in and with it the sky had become slate grey from horizon to horizon. The wind was beginning to drive a drizzling rain into our faces as we headed North back to camp. "You guys go on around the slough," I said to my buddies. "I'm going to cut through and meet you on the other side. Maybe I can jump a deer." As pre-arranged, I waited until they had time to get to the end of the slough before I headed into it. That way, if I spooked a buck, they might get a shot at him. On the other occasions, we had heard deer crashing the length of the slough before exploding through the palmetto fringe at the end.

Ploughing into those tall, dense palmettoes was no easy job. There is a continuous border of them that separates the open grassy pinelands from hardwoods of the slough. You must penetrate thirty to fifty yards of this transition zone in order to reach the taller underbrush and the hardwood trees. Once past the barrier, however, things "open up" and its much easier traveling....and ever so quieter. The rainy season had ended a couple of months ago and what would then have been a foot or two of water was now an often-used animal trail. The tiny little depressions their feet left behind were gradually filling up as each caught its portion of drops dripping from the leaves above.

I hated to fight those palmettoes again so soon. That was ahead of me if I went out the other side so I decided to still hunt for a while. "If I turn left and follow the run of the slough, then I can 'swing a ninety' to the right when I want to work my way out and head toward camp," I said to myself. Turn I did. It was quiet now and all I could hear was the whisper of the wind in the trees and soft "Split-Splat" of raindrops as they fell on the leaves above, re-collected themselves and fell to Earth. This was my reward for passing through the palmetto curtain and I was going to enjoy it for a while before leaving.

I don't know how long I stayed in the slough, but suddenly I began to notice that darkness was settling in. "Better make my right turn", I thought, "and head for camp." Then I noticed that it was a little colder and that the rain was picking up. My hat was saturated, too, and cold water had started dripping down inside the neck of my poncho. "Wow," I murmured to myself, "that campfire will sure feel good." I cursed the palmettoes til soon I was on higher ground looking for the old familiar landmarks that would guide me to camp.

There should have been that firebreak running parallel to the slough and then I'd hit scrub oaks marking the white sand ridge. I'd follow that ridge to the main trail and then head West to camp. None of the signs were where they should have been! I didn't recognize a single thing. "I'm lost!" I said it out loud as though some kind and benevolent super being would hear me and lead me by the hand to that warm fire I envisioned. The "being" never materialized, though, but what was manifest was more rain and wind. Before I panicked, I recalled that the wind had been in our faces and was out of the North; the slough was to our left as we walked back together. It seemed to make sense to me to face the wind and locate North. When I did, the slough was still on my left. Had I come out on same side I had entered?

Darkness was closing around me now; I was cold, wet, and tired. At least I knew I had to head North. Soon I saw the most welcome sight of my life...flashlights! Then I heard a signal shot coming from the same direction. My buddies had gotten concerned and were out searching for me. It wasn't long before we were all back in camp talking about the lesson we (but mainly me) had learned...the hard way.

"What did you wish for most of all when you realized you were lost?" Ed asked the question as if he was ready to make out an emergency list. Indeed, he was! He was preparing then and there to make a list of minimum essentials to carry along even on brief sorties into the woods. Later we decided also to become familiar with a limited number of native edible plants. "Well," I began, "the first thing I thought of was getting dry and warm. I kept picturing you guys back at camp sitting under the tarp warming your hands and feet by the campfire." Thus our list began...dry matches, a dry striking surface and a couple of candles for light. We decided on the candles for two reasons. First, there are no batteries to run down or bulbs to burn out; second, a small portion of a candle could be placed in the middle of tinder to form the makings of a fire. Kitchen matches and a small strip of #200 sandpaper in a waterproof container would assure fire-making ability. A compass took natural 4th place, so naturally we added that to our list.

"What else did you put on your wish list?" Mike asked. Shelter was my next concern. Here, I stubbornly held out for a poncho. You can wear it or you can tie the neck shut and make a shelter out of it. All agreed, but we opted for the old army type with snaps on the sides and grommets in each corner. They make a great lean-to which will not leak. All you need to do is stake down one side and tie the other side to nearby trees or to forked sticks. If two people are lost together, two ponchos will snap together to make a comfortable tent. That made two other items manditory: a small hand ax and a small ball of stout twine. I've done quite a bit of primitive camping and nothing is more handy than stout cord for all sorts of odd jobs. We settled on a hatchet in preference to a hunting knife for obvious reasons. They can be used to chop, of course, but they also cut, pound stakes, split wood, make chips, and with practice, clean game...we all carry a small pocket knife, anyway.

We rounded out our list of minimum essentials with a small canteen of water, some insect repellant and an old bandaid box with some bandaids, gauze and a tube of antibiotic salve. Mike said he preferred to substitute a snake-bite kit. His thinking was that it contained all the above plus tourniquet, suction cup, razor blade, etc....just in case. First aid kits are a personal thing anyway. If you put ten hunters in a room and asked them what they'd prefer, you'd get ten different responses.

Whenever I trek into the woods now, I strap a small Armytype musette bag on my back and in it or on it you can find all the emergency items previously mentioned. Sometimes I cram in one or two other items such as a turkey call, an apple, a candy bar, a dry change of socks, a small pair of binoculars, depending on the nature of the trip and how long I think I'll be out in the woods. Always, though, I'll carry my minimum basic essentials for emergency purposes.

Having completed a basic "needs" list, we began to compile our list of native edible plants. The literature on plants for survival is replete with recommendations. Probably none is more complete than *Wild Plants for Survival in South Florida* by Julia F. Morton. Our problem was to formulate a list of plants which we would recognize easily, which would provide sustenance all year round, and which we could eat uncooked. We don't carry pots, pans, and tableware in our packs and, somehow, we don't expect to have to survive more than a day or two. In addition, we don't want to have to look for something that is seasonal.

Most everybody recognizes a Cabbage Palm when they see it and they are ubiquitous in Florida. "Heart of Palm" even appears or menus of fancy restaurants, but have you ever tried to cut out the growing bud of a palm? Even though they are the official state tree and harvesting them is frowned upon, I'm sure the law enforcement people would forgive you if it meant your survival. More plentiful than cabbage palms, however, are scrub palmettoes and saw palmettoes. The growing buds of both palmettoes are just as palatable as swamp cabbage but much smaller...ie, they are easier to obtain but you get less for your efforts. The berries of both cabbage palm and palmettoes, when ripe, may be eaten raw. Obviously, the berries are seasonal, but the hearts are there all year' round.

Often found growing on cabbage palms as well as hardwood trees is the Smilax vine. You can't hardly go into the woods without seeing a vine that has leathery, shiny, oblong to pear-shaped leaves. Smilax also has recurved thorns on the stem and sometimes on the undersides of the leaf; a common name is bullbrier or briar vine. If you trace the vine back to the Earth and dig up its potato-like root, you can eat the young two to three foot shoots growing out of it. Tracing the vine away from the root you may find loose clumps of black berries on it. They can be eaten raw, too.

While in the woods and looking at vines, check for wild grapevines. They are almost as prolific as bullbrier. Most everyone recognizes bird grapes and caloosa grapes by their heart-shaped leaves. If you cut out a section of the stem and suck on it the sap will quench your thirst. Don't bother to look for bunches of grapes, though, they are sesonal and the birds will beat you to them every time. However, if you are lucky enough to find any, they are edible but bland to taste.

Near the edge of hammocks where they meet the typical pine and palmetto flatlands, you may find thick growths of bracken fern. It is readily recognized by its many-branched leaves. The young uncoiling shoots called fiddleheads are edible and nutritious, if and only if, you trim the woody base and growing tip off. Also, its advisable to rub off the hairs that are growing out of the remaining stem.

Another edible fern is the largest native fern of Florida...the leather fern. It is usually found growing in the shade along the many drainge ditches or near the edges of swampy areas. Along the edge of brackish water near the coast they can also be found, but one can hardly get lost on Florida's coasts anymore. Leather fern is easily recognized by the huge six to seven foot leaves that are rusty brown on the underneath side. Here, as with bracken fern, the uncoiling new leaves are edible. Unlike bracken, though, the whole stem and fiddlehead is excellent forage.

Marshy places and swamps furnish a veritable smorgasbord for the lost hunter. Not only can you find leather ferns nearby, but there are a host of other edible plants. Two that are easily recognized are pickerel weed and "swamp spaghetti," or Sagittaria. They both grow from two to four feet high and have spear-shaped leaves. Pickerel weed has blue, two-lobed flowers whereas, the Sagittaria has three-petalled white flowers. Swamp spaghetti gets its name, no doubt, from the white mass of roots it produces. Bunches are easily pulled out of the soft mud, dunked in the water several times to wash off, and eaten raw. Pickerel weed produces seeds on its flower stalk in the Fall. These may be eaten as you pick them, but are seasonal. They are only mentioned here so that differences between the two plants may be noted. Other swamp foods are cattails and sawgrass. In both cases, the white, young growth is tender and edible without cooking. The heart of overlapping bases of saw grass and the tender leaf bases of catails are both food sources. Most everyone knows cattails when they see them; saw grass is readily recognized by its five to six-foot high leaves which carry saw-like "teeth" the length of the main veins.

One final plant had to be included on our list...the prickly pear cactus. Obviously, it must be handled with care, but all parts are useful. By cutting a small forked stick to hold the fruit, spines should be scraped off and then the skin should be peeled. The remaining pulp may be eaten raw. The joints, as the main stem sections are called, may be eaten raw just like the prickly pear, or they are more tasty when roasted, like marshmellows. More important to remember, however, is that the raw pulp of a catcus joint has medicinal qualities. It may be applied directly to a wound as a poultice to aid healing. The cactus is truly a woodsman's friend, although you may not think so if you bump against one.

After thinking it over, my buddies, Mike and Ed, and I consider my getting lost was fortunate. It caused us to think through what we should have already considered before we ever went hunting. It's something every hunter ought to consider before the fact rather than after it. Our list of emergency articles may differ from yours, but we feel they are adequate for us. The indigenous plants may not suit other hunters and definitely are not appropriate for other areas of our country; however, again, we selected easily recognized, non-seasonal flora that can be found throughout Florida and can be eaten as you pick, and we kept our list to a minimum. We feel secure as we wander in the woods, now. Do you?

GLOSSARY FOR CHAPTER VIII

1. Firebreak—a wide, ploughed furrow is frequently placed between a wooded area and an adjacent grassy field. Its purpose is to stop the spread of a field fire, if one should start accidently or if the land owner should start a controlled burn, and keep the fire from reaching the woods. Such a furrow is called a firebreak.
2. Flora—See Glossary for Chapter I.
3. Hammock—see Glossary for Chapter II.
4. Indigenous Plants—plants that are native to an area. (as indigenous fauna applies to native animals). Flora and fauna that have escaped from captivity or have been introduced to an area are referred to as "exotics."
5. Slough—a long, narrow depression in a relatively flat area and, being lower than the surrounding terrain, is usually wetter. By its very nature, it provides an excellent environment for swampy-type plants to abound, such as water oaks, maples, cypress trees, cabbage palms and the real (ilex) hollies.

CHAPTER IX
FROM RIVER-PEBBLES TO LAND-PEBBLES

The scars are almost undiscernable now but the spectre of those old floating steam dredges loomed around every bend in the river. Echoes of clanking machinery, puffing steam engines, and the raucous voices of the old phosphate miners seemed to richochet back and forth between the walls of vegetation. What a contrast those old "boom" days of the late 1800's must have been in comparison to the serene and solitary canoe trail of today. Jimbo and I had launched our canoe just East of Ft. Meade, Florida, to enjoy drifting down the Peace River for a ways and, just maybe, fish a little along the way. "The Peace River sure is well named," Jim said. "It's so relaxing and the scenery is so beautiful that I almost hope no fish bite."

"Real in your line, then," I replied. "You mentioned the name 'Peace River,' but did you know this same peaceful, pristine canoe trail is the heart of a larger piece of Florida called 'Bone Valley?'" Well, Jim allowed as how he didn't, but that he knew I'd tell him whether he wanted to hear it or not, so he reeled in his line and settled down on the bottom of the canoe.

"What is Bone Valley?" he asked, leading me along. "It sounds as though it might be an old Florida frontier graveyard."

"It's a sort of graveyard, I guess, but not for people," I replied. "Rather, it is a geological formation deposited tens of millions of years ago at a time when this whole part of Florida was covered by ancient seas. It's called, 'Bone Valley,' because when phosphate was discovered in the area and the miners began to dredge and dig for phosphate ore numerous fossilized animal bones, especially those of birds, were also dredged up with the river-pebbles. Piecing together the story told by the fossils, geologists and paleontologists are fairly certain that where we are right now, floating down the Peace River, was a part of an esturine habitat. There was probably a low shoreline to the east and north surrounded by an expansive tidal flat. Dotted throughout the shallows were numerous tree-covered islands of various size and farther out to sea the ocean bottom sloped downward til at greater depths it formed a continental shelf."

"How can fossils tell those guys all that?" Jimbo asked. Answering his question, I explained that there has been a great deal of study of fossilized bird remains from Bone Valley. All the ancient bones that they have been able to find are the remains of species of aquatic birds. They are extinct species, but, those extinct birds are so similar to living species that they can be classified with them and, it can fairly well be assumed that they probably had identical habits. For example, the fossilized bones of shore birds such as sandpipers, herons, flamingoes and sea ducks have been identified in great numbers. Also identified in fairly large numbers are birds that live farther out from shore but within sight of land such as cormorants. In lesser numbers the remains of such open water birds such as albatross, gannets and boobies have been found. Today, modern descendants of most of the species gather on or near shore and nest in large colonies, or rookeries, during mating season; and also, today, shore birds inhabit the rookeries, at any given time, in much greater numbers than open water birds. In other words, fossils of aquatic birds living close to land as well as far out to sea have been uncovered in Bone Valley in about the same ratio as similar species are found in rookeries today.

Jim stopped me cold. Just as I was trying to put everything in a logical order he asked what all this had to do with phosphate and why phosphate was so important that it would bring about a wild "gold rush" style stampede to Florida to mine it. To answer his first question, I explained that the chemical element, phosphorous, is an essential building block of all living (organic) things. The whole inheritance mechanism (i.e., genetic material in the nucleus of every living cell) requires the presence of phosphorous. Phosphorous is also a part of the process of each cell whereby new cell material is manufactured as the organism grows. It also aids cells in storing and releasing energy as they perform their life functions.

Other chemicals are essential to life as well. For example, Nitrogen is also a part of the complex genetic material in the nucleus and it is the chemical basis for amino acid formation which is an essential component of protein; Potassium plays a vital role in the processes of digestion and respiration and it helps maintain the necessary level of acidity or alkalinity in living systems; Magnesium helps living things utilize phosphates and it, like potassium, is a catalyst in digestion and respiration. Calcium is the primary building block of cell walls for plants and supportive structure such as shell and bone in animals. These are only a few of the many chemical elements found in nature that are important constituents of living things.

The whole food chain of life in the seas begins with minute organisms called plankton absorbing soluble forms of elements such as phosphorous, nitrogen, potassium, etc. from the water and synthesizing, or putting them together, in a different chemical form. Larger animals feed on the plankton and in turn become food for still larger aquatic life forms. The birds were apparently the "top of the food chain" because there were no larger animals to feed on them. Surrounding the rockeries the seas were rich in minerals from the bird droppings-or guano. In such a mineral-rich medium, the plankton would thrive and multiply and their success in life would attract the larger forms that feed on the minute organisms. They, in turn, would attract more birds from greater distances.

As this occurs year after year for hundreds of thousands, even millions, of years the resulting sediment on the bottom of the shallow sea would be a conglomerate of a limely mud, calcareous sand, bone and shell fragments. These are the very ingredients necessary for the information of limestone. Furthermore, if the minerals were deposited faster than they could be absorbed back into the mineral cycle, then different sorts of limestone would be present. There would be calcite, the ordinary limestone containing calcium from shell fragments; there would be dolomite, a form of limestone with magnesium as a part of its make-up; and there would be phosphitic limestone which has phosphate chemically bound into its structure.

"You've answered why phosphate is here," Jim said. "I think I can tell why it's important. If phosphate is an essential part of plants and animals, then they must be mining it primarily for use in fertilizer."

"That's correct," I replied, "and most of the phosphate found in nature is found in the form of phosphate rock, and in the form of rock, it is not absorbed by plants. Therefore, it must be processed into a soluble form. Just to show how scarce phosphate ore is, it is estimated that Florida produces about eighty per cent of our nation's phosphate and about twenty per cent of the world's. If it continues to be mined at the present rate, there is enough in the deposits of Florida to last more than 250 years."

"That's a lot of fertilizer!" said Jim.

Phosphate in the form of river-pebbles was obtained by dredging the Peace River for some twenty years from 1887 to 1908. In the middle of this short span of time, the miners changed their tactics to strip mining in the whole Bone Valley area. It wasn't long, however, before the mining companies discovered a high presence of phosphate in the layer of limestone situated just below the Bone Valley Formation. This lower stratum called the Hawthorne Formation, was much more extensive in area and much thicker in depth than Bone Valley limestone. The percent of phosphate is considerably less in some areas of the Hawthorne limestone, though. In fact, they find quite extensive lens-shaped deposits of pure calcite which has no phosphate in it at all. A logical conclusion is that, as the ocean floor heaved up (or ocean level went down) and the various limestone layers became exposed to weathering, magnesium and minerals leached downward from the Bone Valley Formation to the Hawthorne Formation and combined with the original calcite to form dolomite and phosphitic limestone.

The Bone Valley Formation lies within a limited area close to the Peace River. It extends from near Bartow at its Northern limits to a point somewhere near Arcadia at its Southern end. The Hawthorne Formation, however, extends well over 3,000 square miles and encompasses the major land portions of six counties in West Central Florida. In those areas where Hawthorne limestone is not covered by the Bone Valley Formation, it is covered by a sandy to clay-filled soil. In some places near the axis of Florida, the Hawthorne Formation crops out of the ground. To the south in Manatee and Sarasota counties, it is about 350 feet deep.

Most strip mines are around the Bartow area where the Hawthorne Formation is about twenty feet to thirty feet below the surface. What the mining companies have to do is strip the top soil down to the phosphate bearing limestone. They are required to store this soil called "overburden" so they can replace it when they are finished mining. After they have stripped this upper layer of dirt, the phosphitic limestone is removed by huge draglines. It is dumped into other huge pits and washed to separate the phosphate ore or land-pebbles from the sands and clays and non-phosphitic limestone. The ore is then stored and dried in preparation for shipment to processing plants. The wash water with its sand, clay, and slit is sent to another huge settling basin where the finer particles will settle to the bottom. The clean water at the top of the settling basin is drawn off and reused for washing more ore. The sediment that is left in the basin is reprocessed so that ore-bearing particles are removed and the remainder is saved with the overburden for land reclamation.

"Land Reclamation!" said Jimbo. It shocked me because he'd been sitting in the bottom of our canoe with his eyes closed. I thought he had been sleeping and hadn't heard much of what I had said.

"Yes," I replied and continued. "Before the mining companies even strip the first layer they have to submit a plan showing how the land will look when they are finished. In the past, they have put the mined land, back into pasture or subdivisions with lakefront property where their huge mining, washing, and holding pits were. Recently, however, guidelines set up by Florida Game and Freshwater Fish Commission require that recreational game and fishing areas be included in the land reclamation plans."

"They have to go through a lot just to get Phosphate for fertilizer, don't they?" Jim asked.

"Well, theirs is a messy operation," I replied. "They gouge out huge, unsightly tracts of land; they use tremendous amounts of water; and they pollute the air with dust from the piles of ore and toxic emissions from their processing plants. Not only is the state concerned with land reclamation, but there are stringent controls on where they get the water they use and where they put it when they are finished; the state also monitors the air pollutants as well."

"It's still hard for me to believe," Jimbo said, "that all those huge piles of dirt and ore around Bartow and Lake Wales will look like this some day!" He waved his arm in an arc like a Shakespearian actor and included the clear, flowing water of the peace River enclosed on its flanks with some of the most beautiful wild country in Florida. I had to agree.

GLOSSARY FOR CHAPTER IX

1. Acidity—technically, acids give up hydrogen ions in solution (or when mixed with water). Practically, they are sour or tart to the taste such as the citric acids in lemon juice, oxilic acid in green apples, and acetic acid in vinegar. It is extremely important that living tissue be able to control the strength of acid solutions within their tissues.
2. Alkalinity—alkaline substances are the chemical opposites of acids in that they give up hydroxyl ions in solution rather than hydrogen ions like acids. Practically, alkaline substances can act to neutralize acids to form salty water. They are bitter to the taste and they usually are slippery to touch like soap.
3. Amino Acid— the structural units from which large protein molecules are synthesized. The amino acid molecules can exhibit properties of both acids and bases (alkalines) and can, therefore, combine with each other to form huge chains of atoms formed together into one molecule.
4. Axis of Florida—see Glossary for Chapter VI
5. Bone Valley—lies in the heart of the phosphate region of Florida and includes parts of Polk, Hardee, and De Soto counties. It is about halfway between the Kissimmee River (also known as C-38) and the Gulf of Mexico. The Bone Valley Formation refers to the strata of limestone just below the surface of the Earth in the Bone Valley area.
6. Bone Valley Formation—see Bone Valley in this Glossary.
7. Calcareous—see Glossary for Chapter IV.
8. Calcareous Sand—sand, the particles of which are mainly composed of calcite. (see also calcite and sand.)
9. Calcite—see Glossary for Chapter III.
10. Calcium—one of the primary chemical elements of the earth. It is classified by chemists as a metallic substance, because it reacts in chemical reactions like beryllium, magnesium, and other metallic elements.
11. Catalyst—see Glossary for Chapter III.
12. Clay—classified by geologists as a type of soil made up of extremely fine particles about a ten-thousandth of an inch

across. Minerals most common in "clayey" soils are aluminum and silicon. (See also Sand and Silt in this Glossary.)
13. Conglomerate—one in which easily distinguishable fragments of rock are cemented together. The fragments are usually of a different type of rock than the cementing material, which is usually a sedimentary type of rock or an igneous type of rock such as lava from a volcano.
14. Digestion—the process in living organisms whereby insoluble (undissolved) forms of food are changed to soluble form (in solution) so that the food may absorbed and transported or circualted to other parts of the organism.
15. Dolomite (or Dolomitic Limestone)—this a form of limesote which contains the element magnesium in its chemical make up. Dolomite also has a different crystalline structure from calcite, the more common form of limestone.
16. Estaurine Habitat (or ecosystem)—characterized by the flow of tidal waters through it with the changes of the tide. Usually it is crisscrossed with a myriad of channels cut by the flow of water as it comes and goes. An estaurine habitat has its own typical flora and fauna, such as the sedges, salt grasses, chord grasses, fidler crabs, etc.
17. Food Chain—as naturalists use the term, it refers to the "pecking order" of animals in an ecosystem with regard to their eating preference...who eats whom, so to say. Some of the animals are plant eaters; others are carnivorous. Practically all of both groups enter into the food chain some way with smaller animals being the prey to larger ones and so on up the line until there are a select few left of the largest. This latter group is called the top of the food chain.
18. Fort Meade—a modern city located in the southern part of Polk County. It is also the site of one of the forts built during the Second Indian Wars. (See Glossary for Chapter I.)
19. Fossil—see Glossary for Chapter III.
20. Genetic Material—all living things transmit their traits and unique characteristics through an inheritance mechanism that is called Genetic Material; it is composed of highly complex molecules that can be found in the nucleii of living cells.
21. Geologist—a scientist who studies rocks, rock formations, and overburden material. Through such studies the

Geologist proposes how the Earth was formed and how it has changed since its formation.

22. Guano—in a rookery where large numbers of birds congregate during mating season, their excrement accumulates on the ground or in the shallow waters below the many nests. Over a period of many years, hundreds of thousands of years, the excrement can accumulate in great quantities. When it does so, it is referred to as Guano.

23. Hawthorne Formation (sometimes called Hawthorn Formation, without the "e")—strata of limestone formed in the middle Miocene period (see Glossary for Chapter III.) The Hawthorne Formation is a layer if limestone, lying just below the Bone Valley Formation and is much more extensive in area than the latter.

24. Land-Pebbles—phosphitic rock frequently dug up miners. The term originally was applied to pebble-sized phosphitic rock, mined in the Bone Valley area near the Peace River at the beginning of the "Phosphate Rush" in the late 1800s.

25. Limestone—see Glossary for Chapter II.

26. Magnesium—a metallic element that reacts chemically in a similar fashion to beryllium and calcium. Its presence in Dolomite could have occurred when the dolomite originally formed or the magnesium could have leached down through the layers of limestone and replaced the calcium already there. This latter process is called "dolomitization."

27. Nitrogen—exists most abundantly in nature as a gas which comprises about eighty per cent of our atmosphere. In this form it is very stable and not readily available to plants or animals. The chemical forms by which it can be absorbed from the soil by plants are compounds which include hydrogen and oxygen along with the nitrogen such as ammonia, nitrates, and nitrites.

28. Nucleus—in a living cell it controls most of the processes that occur within the cell. It also contains the inheritance mechanism, i,e., the genetic material (see elsewhere in this Glossary) by which the cell reproduces and retains its own characteristics.

29. Overburden—in this chapter, overburden refers to whatever is on top of the phosphitic limestone. In Bone Valley the overburden is the Bone Valley Formation; elsewhere the

overburden of the Hawathorne Formation is a mixture of silty, sandy and clayey soils.
30. Paleontologist—see Glossary for Chapter V.
31. Phosphate—part of a chemical compound that exists in rock form in nature, combined with a metallic element, such as calcium or magnesium.
32. Phosphate Rock (or Phosphitic Rock)—a form of limestone that has compounds of phosphorous as a part of its chemical makeup. (see also land-pebbles and river-pebbles in this Glossary.)
33. Phosphorous—a highly reactive element in its purest form. It is so reactive, however, that it is not found in nature in that form. Its importance to living organisms cannot be over-emphasized since phosphorous is a major constituent of genetic material and is needed by every living cell to aid in respiration, digestion, reproduction, and other processes.
34. Plankton—see Glossary for Chapter V.
35. Potassium—like phosphorous, potassium is essential to the processes of living cells. It acts as catalyst in such cell activities as respiration and synthesis of protein. There is some question as to its precise part played in the cell activities, but cells cannot perform them as efficiently without it.
36. Protein—highly complex molecules that are the building blocks of living cell material called protoplasm. As an example of a protein's complexity, there are well over 700 atoms in each molecule of the common protein called egg white.
37. River-Pebbles—the term was used by the early phosphate miners in Florida to refer to the pebble-sized ore that they dredged up from the bottom of the Peace River. It was the discovery of these phosphitic pebbles that started the mining of phosphate in Florida.
38. Respiration—the process whereby living cells utilize digested food in the release of energy so that they can perform their various cellular activities.
39. Rookery—a place where great numbers of aquatic birds congregate during the mating season. Sometimes the population is all one species of bird; at other times several species will nest in the same rookery.

40. Sand—geologists classify soil by the size of its particles. The particles of sand are produced by weathering of rock and organically produced hard structures such as shell and chitinous material. When such materials are reduced to particles less than about a tenth of an inch in size by the motion of the waves, but are still larger than about a fiftieth of an inch, they are technically classified as sand. (See also Clay and Silt in the Glossary for this chapter.)
41. Silt—a soil that is composed of particles smaller than sand, but larger than Clay. (See also Sand and Clay in the Glossary for this Chapter.)
42. Strip Mining—a type of mining where the over burden (i.e., top soil and material between the soil and the ore to be mined) is removed from over the ore; the ore is then mined; and the overburden is replaced. The process leaves huge piles of ore and overburden strewn around and it also requires that large gouges in the Earth be present in the area.
43. Synthesis—the process of putting things together. It is used in this chapter to describe how living organisms can absorb or ingest materials out of their environment, digest them, combine them into more and more complex substances, and ultimately convert them into its own living tissue.

CHAPTER X
TABBY ON THE STREETS

On July 10, 1821 Florida became a territory of the United States. Throughout both Eastern and Western provinces, the Spanish flag was lowered and the Stars and Stripes raised. In St. Augustine the capitol city of the Eastern Province, Col. Robert Bulter, who was General Andrew Jacksons' personal representative, assumed command of Castillo de san Marcos; while Spanish Governor, Jose Coppinger, was relieved of his duties. There was much discussion in Washington about whether or not President James Monroe was in command of all his faculties as he supported the acquisition.

To most critics the land was considered a quagmire of swamps that were filled with mosquitos and renegade Indians. President Monroe, however, saw it as an opportunity for the United States to have harbors both on the Atlantic Ocean and the Gulf of Mexico. This would mean that the young United States controlled the Eastern seaboard of North America from the Carolinas and Georgia all the way around to the State of Louisiana. Each year in July, St. Augustine celebrates the "changing of the flag" and so my wife and I resolved to be there.

Upon our arrival at the quaint town, we soon discovered that for some strange reason, they were celebrating the Spanish takeover from the British, which also happened in July, but some forty odd years earlier than the American acquisition...and the significance of this occasion was that the British got out of the new world altogether. Be that as it may, Ceil and I had arrived in St. Augustine a couple of days before the ceremonies so we would know our way around by the time the crowds filled the streets. One of the best ways to acquaint yourself with the town is to ride a tour train. They take you to all points of historical interest for a nominal price. Soon we were aboard and as we rode along, we heard the guide saying over the loudspeaker"....the oldest city...,...the first school....,....the first house...," and so on and so on. After a while, it seemed as though everything in St. Augustine was "the first something or other."

As the tour train drove into the entrance of the Fountain of Youth, I caught the statement "...and here on both sides of the entrance is a tabby and oyster shell wall built in 17--." I didn't catch the whole date because his words were drowned out by curiosity. "'Tabby,' I must have misunderstood," I said to myself. When the train stopped for all of us to sip and regain our youth, I walked to the driver and asked him what the wall was made of. I said "I didn't hear you clearly."

"Tabby," he replied, "is a mixture of equal parts of sand, lime, and oyster shells. It's what most of the homes were made of during the Spanish colonial period." This was followed by a brief history lesson in which he explained that Florida was a Spanish Colony for about 200 years until the Treaty of Paris in 1763. At that time, it became a British Colony. About twenty years later, the Spanish got it back, again by treaty, and sold it to the United States in 1821.

Toward the end of the first two hundred years, after the town had been sacked and burned again and again, tabby became an important construction material. I thought to myself, "All those 'firsts' I've been told about weren't really first." The first buildings were burned not just by the British in 1702, but by Indians and privateers when the Spanish lived there and by the Spanish and French when the first human inhabitants, the Timucuan Indians, called it Seloy. Those really and truly first buildings of the Timucua were built of logs and woven sticks covered by thatching from cabbage palm fronds.

As the early Spanish explorers befriended the Timucua they, too, built living quarters patterned after the Indian huts-logs and sticks with thatched walls and roofs. They had to use the raw materials at hand for there was no other material available. The Spanish Colony grew and its leaders wanted better living quarters as well as a fort for protection. To satisfy these demands, wood was imported and a few wooden structures were built. By that time the Spanish had driven away the Timucua, occupied their thatched huts, and stolen their stores of food. The town was attacked by Indians, who were now hostile, and burned. It was rebuilt with wood and thatch huts and this time a wooden fort was included. Again it was attacked and burned by the British in 1586 and then again by pirates some eighty years later. Driven back, the pirates vowed to return.

The Spanish governor's report of this latter attack prompted Queen Regent Mariana to order construction of Casillo de san Marcos-a fort which still stands today. The fort was to be built with tabby and coquina rock from nearby Anastasia Island. Large kilns were imported from Spain to make lime out of the mounds of oyster shells left by the Timucua. The oyster shells were crushed to a fine powder and heated in the ovens to about 1800°F.. Heat drives off all the moisture and the carbon dioxide from the shell powder; what remains is quick lime. When quick lime is mixed with water again an carbon dioxide from the atmosphere, heat and water are given off slowly and it hardens, or sets, to its original state. The presence of sand speeds up the process and adds strength to the tabby; the addition of whole shell or rock to the mixture provides filler material, or aggregate as it's called.

It is interesting to note that the cementing properties of quick lime, sand and aggregate had been known by early civilizations almost worldwide. The process of making modern Portland Cement wasn't patented until 1824. The raw materials from which Portland Cement is made include everything used in making tabby with a few other things added such as: limestone, coquina shell, marl shell, clay, shale rock, and iron ore in small amounts. The mixture is pulverized, heated, and the resulting clinkers are pulverized again. At this point Gypsum is added and the resulting mixture is Portland Cement. These modern refinements have all been added to help control setting time and strength of the final product.

Just before the patent was given for Portland Cement in England, John Sewell, a pioneer settled in Miami, had discovered yet another early form of cementing rock. As he said in his memories the discovery was quite "... by accident instead of hard study or great wisdom." Miami Oölite (limestone) had been broken up and scattered where a sidewalk was to go. Laborers had tamped it down to make it level and smooth to walk on. No sooner had all this been done when wind kicked up off the Biscayne Bay and started blowing the powder all over. The annoyed Sewell had his workers water down the powdered limestone to prevent it from all blowing away. "Next morning," he said "I went over to see how my walk was getting along and there it was all set up hard like cement..."

East, across the bay from where Castillo de san Marcos was to be built, is a barrier island the Spanish called Anastasia Island. It was known to have large deposits of Coquina Rock which has the unique property of being easily cut into blocks. Once the blocks are removed and exposed to weathering of the atmosphere, they harden into solid impervious rock. The process is very similar to the cementing of Sewell's Miami Oölite limestone. When the queen ordered construction of the fort, the presence of both conquina rock and oyster mounds for tabby were known. Earlier Spanish settlers had not taken advantage of the two materials because of the difficulty and expenses in obtaining each. When the Queen backed up her orders, however, with both money and laborers, the two new building materials became more plentiful, although they were reserved for the Castillo until its completion.

The Brittish attacked and sacked St. Augustine in 1702, however, the completed Castillo de san Marcos did its job. People and crops and domestic animals were all herded to the safety of its thick coquina walls. There they remained as the battle raged.

Although the fort was undaunted in the siege, the entire town was a shambles, and complete reconstruction of the buildings began soon after the British departed. Some homes of the laborers were hastily built using any available materials left from the burning. Logs, boards, sticks, canvas, and thatching were all employed in hasty fashion to provide cover from the elements. Thus housed, workers began to construct permanent residences for the more affluent members of the community.

As a general rule, these more permanent homes had coquina rock or tabby foundations. Inside the foundation, tabby floors were poured and on top of the foundation tabby walls were built. With the use of form boards, the walls were built in layers until the first floor was completed. If there was to be a second floor, it was usually built of wood. Roofs were both thatched and shingled. Door and window openings were often covered by curtains and wooden grates or gates. Panel doors and glazed windows were still a century or so away. Some of the more expensive houses were built of Coquina rock cemented together with tabby, but there were few of these.

The Spanish handed the Keys to Castillo de san Marcos to the British in 1764 as a result of the Treaty of Paris. When they did, they also gave the British and inventory of buildings which comprised the town of St. Augustine. Their tally showed that about 350 homes had been built. There were stone houses with tabby floors, tabby and wood houses, and wooden houses with thatched roofs. Some of these structures are still standing and it is these that are pointed out by the tour guides as being "the oldest" or "the first" of whatever they are explaining. What they really mean is that those buildings are "the oldest ones that are still standing" or "the first buildings built after the British raid in 1702."

While St. Augustine was under British rule, a few of the spanish citizens remained. The homes of those who left were occupied by the British and as the whole town population grew, new buildings were built. Homes built by the British were patterned after the architectural styles of the Carolinas and were markedly different from the casas of the Spanish...they were the typical 16' x 24' frame houses with plank flooring, clapboard walls and shingle roofs. A few of these are still standing and are "first" or "oldest" in their own way.

Ceil and I completed the entire tour of St. Augustine and decided to go back to what they call "the old City Gate." It is the entrance to the original historical part of town and is now the location of numerous quaint shops and tourist attractions. As we walked up St. George Street we could feel antiquity penetrating our entire beings. We were surrounded by the old wooden buildings with their shingle roofs. There were stone houses with tabby and oyster shell walls enclosing their yards. Each now contains one of the many souvenir shops. Ceil and I finally entered one of the shops to soak up some inside atmosphere. The lady behind the counter was dressed in an old fashioned ankle length dress to suit the occasion. "Isn't it exciting," I asked "that the Changing of the Flags will be celebrated day after tomorrow? The Governor will be here; the cannons will be fired; the British and Spanish soldiers will shoot their muskets in mock battle; and, finally, there'll be the Grand Ball!"

Without even looking up she answered "They're always celebrating something here. It's good for business, I guess."

GLOSSARY FOR CHAPTER X

1. Aggregate rock—made of components that are readily distinguishable from each other and can easily be separated from it and from each other without the use of any complex processes.
2. Anastasia Island—the barrier island just across the intercoastal waterway from the city of St. Augustine. It was the site of the Coquina Rock mines when the Spanish were building Castillo de San Marcos.
3. Castillo de San Marcos—the great stone fort, built by the Spanish, to protect the city of St. Augustine from the British, the Indians and other marauders during the Spanish rule. It was built in the 1600's and was never conquered in battle. It is still standing.
4. Coquina Rock—a form of limestone that is made from a sediment composed of great quantities of broken Coquina shell, coral, and other calcareous debris. When the overburden is removed and the Coquina Rock is exposed, it can be readily cut into blocks. Once these blocks are exposed to atmospheric weathering they harden, or set like concrete.
5. Limestone—see Glossary for Chapter II.
6. Oölite—a calcareous form of limestone that occurs in nature as tiny spherical or football-shaped grains called ooliths. Once these ooliths are crushed, tamped in place, and watered down, they will set like concrete. The coastal ridge in the Miami area sits on a huge deposit of oolite and it was so readily available and so easy to work with that many of the first streets and sidewalks were made of it.
7. Portland Cement—Joseph Aspdin was granted a patent in 1824 in England for inventing both the process and the contents that go into the making of Portland Cement. Materials from which it is made can be varied in different amounts so that different setting times, as well as hardness, can be controlled for different uses of the cement.

8. Quick Lime—can be made by heating crushed limestone, shell, or other substances which are made of Aragonite or calcite to a temperature of 1800°F. The heating drives off moisture and causes the calcite to lose carbon dioxide. What is left is a white powder called quick lime. When the quick lime is mixed with sand, water, and any kind of rock or other filler such as shells, the mixture produces a crude form of cement called tabby.
9. Tabby—see Quick Lime in this Glossary.
10. Timucua—like the Ais (See Glossary for Chapter I) and the Caloosa (See Glossary for Chapter IV) a tribe of Indians that inhabited the Northeast part of Florida and the Southeast part of Georgia for thousands of years before the invasion of their territory by both the Europeans and the Seminoles.

APPENDIX

As mentioned in the Preface this section of *Tracks on the Florida Trails* is the summarized proceedings of an open forum planned and conducted by the author. The reader is given the following hypothetical situation to illustrate the concept of carrying capacity. Imagine a rancher raising his cattle an open range-i.e., he has made no improvements other than fencing in his land. He would require about fifteen to twenty five *acres* per *cow*. With improvement such as clearing, planting pasture grass, fertilizing, irrigating, etc., he can increase the carrying capacity of his ranch to fifteen to twenty five *cows* per *acre*. If he adds feeders to supplement the pasture grass diet, he can increase the carrying capacity a little more. Each time he wants to increase the cattle population he must add something to the system. One of the dilemmas created with this process is that each time something is added to increase carrying capacity some of the original character of the total system is destroyed and its very loss will require the addition of still more new technology. Obviously, there are limits to the growth of every system from our rancher's open range to a city or a state....or even a nation!

Having given considerable thought to the problem of population growth in Florida and having wondered if much consideration has been given to it by Florida planners, the author proposed and conducted a forum fostering the exchange of ideas of approximately one hundred business executives from both government and the private sector. What follows are questions posed to the group and a summary of their responses.

Question One. Do you think the relationship between services provided by government and goods and services produced by the private sector will change in a no growth situation?
Summarized Responses:
It was brought out that a steady state economy might be possible at such a time when the resources of an area are no longer

able to support growth. It was not seen to be possible as a result of fiat or governmental intervention. In a democratic system, if the growth potential is there growth will occur. On the other hand, however, when a region is no longer competitive with other regions, and people can get more for their investment elsewhere, they will go where they get the greatest return.

No growth was defined by some groups as meaning no population growth. It was thought that since Gross Regional Product was not necessarily a function of population there could be continued economic growth. This opinion was further supported by the supposition that a population mix could vary even though there were no changes in the total numbers of people.

The relationship between governmental services and those of the private sector would be varied and complex. In government it might be a reduction in demand for some services, but with a variable mix within the population there might be a greater demand for other services. During the time of fluctuation and adjustment the per capita costs of government might rise. For example, since there might be no need to plan for further growth the thrust of planning might be in the area of retrenchment as well as finding new ways to serve the public and improving those services already available. Some services now performed by government might be turned over to the private sector as the need for newer services becomes obvious. In the short-term there might be a significant need for a more centralized government if things become chaotic. It would be necessary to assist people as they relocate, retrain, resettle, and, in general, readjust. A long term effect might call for less governmental involvement as people become more self-reliant and self-sufficient.

In the private sector the impact of no growth might cause a significant revision of the objectives of those industries serving people's changing needs. The construction industry, for example, might have to shift emphasis from building new units to modifying and maintaining units already built or reconstructing outmoded or unused units. A rise in cooperative type organizations might cause less need for large numbers of retail outlets. In the manufacturing of products an increase of "do-it-yourselfers" might necessitate more products to be marketed in kit form. Interestingly, along these same lines, one discussion group thought there might be less emphasis placed on formal and vocational schooling as the trades industry implemented apprenticeship programs.

Question Two. Does no growth necessarily mean that a land-use plan is "in place"?

Summarized Responses:

Each of the discussion groups thought that the basic land-use master plan would have to remain in force. Since current plans are based on growth, they would have to be amended. Some participants foresaw a shift of population concentration to the inner city, whereas growth is now toward the peripheral areas. It was also brought out that shifts in age structure, ethnic mix, and so forth, would require concomitant land-use changes. Furthermore, changes in the relationships between government and private enterprise accompanied with other changes outlined in Question One would require flexible land-use plans. One discussion group foresaw population shifts away from the inner city to satellite, planned, neighborhood, urban communities. Shifts in industrial centers and governmental centers were perceived to accompany the population shifts and dynamic planning was deemed necessary to accomplish the moves.

Question Three. Do you think people's life-style will necessarily change as a result of no growth?

Summarized Responses:

Each discussion group responded differently to this question. One group thought that life-styles would not be altered significantly from the way we now know it. Life-styles change now for various reasons in spite of a "growth" mode. They might change somewhat as a natural turn of events. A "no growth" society may, however, free people up so that they are able to change their life-style as other changes in society occur.

The other discussion groups thought there might be a rather drastic change in life-styles on a short term basis. They differed, however, in their long-range projections: one thought that the changes would be minor after the initial adjustments had been made; the other thought that the drastic changes would persist. All groups agreed that the quality of life would be better.

Some specific examples of change which people may experience in a steady state were: (a) people would become more self-reliant, but at the same time there would be greater cooperation between groups and individuals; (b) there would be smaller living quarters and a higher population density (shift to the inner city) which would require some adaptation; (c) there would be less governmental controls needed because of the increased cooperative spirit; (d) as new neighborhoods are created in the inner city or satellite planned neighborhood, urban communities there would be a new surge of urban (or suburban) planning and renewal; (e) individuals as well as community planners would be faced with fitting old structures and roads, etc., to satisfy new needs; (f) they would be faced with decisions to be made to maximize the use of natural resources; (g) they would be closer to their jobs and to their leisure time activities which would require less commuting time and more public transportation; (h) more leisure time would be devoted to family activities such as gardening, handicraft, build-it-yourself, picnics, etc., and more needs would be fulfilled at home; (i) technology would still be flourishing, however, particularly in the areas of electronics, data processing and information processing so that communication networks would keep communities enlightened about social trends, economic, educational and governmental trends. Sociologically, a no growth situation was perceived to create a social class structure with greater numbers of "haves" and "have-nots" and a diminishing of the middle classes.

Question Four. What effects would no growth have on your particular industry or service area?

Summarized Responses:

The responses to this question are broken down by interest group and/or occupation.

(a) *Government*—a static population would allow the public sector to function better by "catching up" on the planning and providing of services it now offers. It would also provide time for analysis and implementation of services needed but not now offered. Some difficulty might be encountered in justifying budget items. These difficulties might carry over into the tax structure of the area. Both services and the tax support for them would probably have to be justified by complex impact studies or other means rather than population projections. Other effects on government already mentioned earlier in this report would be a short-term increase in the need for more government control followed by less government intervention and more diffused or decentralized government. There would probably be a greater need for cooperation between the public and private sectors as industries compete for a piece of the "static financial pie".

(b) *Construction*—There would be serious problems in this industry as they attempt to transfer emphasis on reconstruction, renovation, conversion, repair, and maintenance activities. The industry would be more competitive and the quality of their product would improve. New design and building techniques would be developed as the demand for more passive architecture becomes greater.

(c) *Real Estate*—The quality of personnel and services would probably improve in the real estate business as they make the shift from making a "fast buck" on the big sales to the slower pace of handling rentals and resales. Personnel would probably have to have more and better training which might make the costs of the service go up. It was predicted that prices of land would go up.

(d) *Tourism*—No groups thought that tourism would be adversely affected although there was some discussion about the availability of natural resources to support random fluctuations in the population as a result of the tourist trade. In general, tourism would remain a mainstay of the economy.

(e) *Agriculture*—Agricultural activities would be greatly effected. It is a large part of the economy presently and was predicted to become even more important. One need seen was for a greater diversity in crops per farmer and for more crops to be consumed locally. Homesites would probably include more vegetable gardens, but, due to the generally small amount of space available, such gardens would not satisfy the demand.

(d) *Transportation and Communication*—There would probably be a greater emphasis on low energy types of transportation for private individuals and a greater need for mass transit systems. With increased use there would be a greater demand for higher quality in the transportation industry and the demand would be met, probably at a higher cost. There would necessarily be a need for a complex communications network with fewer people traveling out of their local community; probably there would also arise a need for more local communication systems such as the neighborhood newspapers.

(g) *Education*—Briefly, it was thought that there would be less emphasis on higher education, that educational programs would emphasize the basic skills of communications, mathematics and citizenship, home skills, and work skills in the service areas and technical areas. Education would also be involved in retraining of people who change occupations as well s upgrading of occupational skills. These latter functions might be assumed by industry itself in the form fo apprenticeship programs and advancement programs.

(h) *Judicial*—It was thought and there would be a reduction in the needs for legal services. With increased cooperative spirit among citizens, criminals activities were projected to decline; with greater emphasis on mass transit, automobile-related traffic cases were predicted to decrease in numbers; civil infractions might increase, however, as well as adjudication of land-use disputes. These were seen to increase as people come in closer contact with each other and as the land-use master plan is revised. Overall, the need for legal services and court action was seen to become less on a long-range basis.

(i) *Manufacturing*—The light manufacturing industry, it was thought, would be affected less than heavy manufacturers; however, there might be differential effects within the light industries. Those companies dealing with oil based products might suffer most--such as paints, plastics, synthetics, and some chemicals. Light industries which manufacture household necessities would probably have fewer problems--particularly if the raw supplies used are from renewable resources or commonly occurring materials.

(j) *Banking and Finance*—With the rise of cooperatives, do-it-yourselfers, and the general self-sufficiency of the people, it was thought that there would be a decline in financial activities in general. Mortgage financing would probably shift to emphasis on re-financing; cash flow would probably be reduced, credit transactions would probably be fewer. Probably the whole investment business would be drastically revised; however it would remain a major part of the economy.

(k) *Retail Sales and Distribution*—It was thought that the retail outlets might be adversely affected. The formation of neighborhood cooperatives and the increase of constructive, home-oriented leisure activities would be an influencing factor. With more effort being put into meeting local demands with local supplies and local natural resources, goods brought into the region might decline. Such a situation would force retailers to re-examine how they fit into the changing scene. Population shifts to the inner city or its satellite, planned-neighborhood, might also require a shift from large chain operation to neighborhood, proprietary stores.

(l) *Medical*—There would still be great emphasis on health and safety. It was seen that this could be a time for "catching up" and improving what services are now available. There might be less need for specialization in the medical field and a return to the old neighborhood, family practice.

Question Five. What course of action should government and industry take so that the effects of no growth would be minimized?

Summarized Responses:

"Effects" in this question were assumed by all discussion groups as "negative effects". Things that the public and private sectors could do to minimize the shock of steady state were mostly governmental responsibilities. Although there is presently a considerable amount of cooperation, it was indicated that this must increase. The government, it was hoped, would: a) embark on a large publicity campaign to assist citizens to see what was happening, why it was happening, and how to adjust to the changing conditions; b) impose controls during the transition to minimize inequities that might occur; c) review licensing and minimum standards to assist in the shift from quantity (for growth) to to quality; d) revise school attendance laws and curricula to adjust for the changing needs indicated earlier; f) review unemployment compensation laws so that displaced persons must receive retraining; g) revise minimum wage laws so that basic labor can be obtained and having jobs can be competitive with remaining unemployed; and, finally, h) concentrate on developing (with the private sector) an organized, rational community plan for "surviving" the transitional phases of the change. Plans should fairly include, as was discussed in other sections, a means of shifting and revising government services and even for government phasing itself out where necessary and for decentralizing itself.

Some of the more generalized conclusions that were presented at the end of the formal forum proceedings are as follows:

1. We must keep in mind that a steady state system means no growth in the total amount of structure or assets (i.e., no net

growth), but this does not mean a stagnant system, for there is continual growth. It is a growth by replacement. In other words, as parts of the system become worn out or senescent (such as roads, buildings, machines, furniture, etc.) they are replaced...new parts of the system are "grown" to replace that which has become senescent. Much like a climax forest, there is not over all growth of the system, but there is growth by replacement. As a tree grows old and dies, it is replaced by a new tree that grows up to take its place.

2. It is important to understand that if there is no growth in the addition of outside resources of a region, and thus in the physical structure of the system, and there *is* growth of population, then the resources, and structure of the region must be divided amongest an increasing population base. Each inhabitant receives less and less as the population grows. Thus "standard of living" suffers.

3. Since money and resources are intricately interwoven in the regional systems of man, a leveling in the availability of those resources will mean a leveling of growth and must also mean a leveling of the capital available for expenditure and investment. If resources remain constant and the availability of money is allowed to increase and inflation will result since more money will circulate for the same amount of resources. Thus, during times when no resources are imported, there should be no increase in the amount of money in circulation.

4. When the supply of money remains constant, there will be little credit. Since there will be no increase in outside resources in the future, there is nothing to lend money against; for only if there is an increasing base is there the possibility of paying back the principal as well as the interest on a loan.

5. As the supplies of local resources decrease and become more costly, labor will play an increasing role in productive processes, and all members of society will be called upon to maintain productivity of the system. Wages may fluctuate at first, but they should stabilize as the system adjusts to lower resource conditions.

6. Imports and exports will play a lesser role in the regional economy as the costs of transportation increase with lower resource availability. Thus a "regionalization" of goods and services (extreme diversity now available) will decline.

7. There may still be some tourism, but at a much reduced

scale, with visitors traveling by mass transit such as trains and ocean going vessels.

8. Since pensions and social security are based on the expectation of increasing economy in the future when the income is paid to recipients, and since there will be no economic increase in the steady state pattern, income to the region will decline. Communities whose economic base is largely derived from these sources will have difficulties in maintaining economic well-being.

9. Industries which rely on local resources (such as solar technology and agricultural industries) will increase in productive output and then level off as the economy becomes more regional. Those industries that are primarily growth industries (i.e., construction) will decline and become more maintenance oriented.

10. Since the State of Florida is increasingly becoming the "gateway" to South America, and since the countries of South America have some large supplies of resources, the economy of Florida could be tied to these countries. Importing and exporting goods to them will increase for a time until these resources decline.

11. Transportation will become more localized, with the majority of travel by mass transportation, bicycles, and walking, as well as other efficient means of transportation. Thus there should not be the need for expansion of super highways and interstate systems. Rail and some water transportation should again become important.

12. As present day air conditioned buildings become senescent they will be replaced by buildings that can be naturally cooled and heated. The very large scale buildings of the downtowns and the beaches will eventually be replaced by smaller scale, more efficient, naturally ventilated structures.

13. The size of the urban population will decrease if inhabitants leave the urban centers for the rural areas. There may be some shift of construction and total structure away from the urban cores to outlying agricultural regions.

14. Cities will be of a more human scale, as they are planned around pedestrian, bicycle, and some small scale vehicle traffic. Green spaces and productive crop areas will become important uses of the urban landscape.

15. Natural wetland ecosystems will be utilized as recycle systems for sewage wastes and as water conservation units. Recycle of materials will continue to increase and become of prime impor-

tance.

16. Housing will utilize more passive heating and cooling systems, with emphasis on solar heating, and natural breezes and forced air for cooling. Natural vegetation will replace exotic landscapes and manicured lawns.

17. As central cities decrease in population size, rural places will increase as the population seeks a more even distribution on the landscape. Mass transportation between central cities and rural places will increase as central cities retain their attraction to social, cultural, and educational centers.

18. As population densities decline, so will the negative consequences of population density such as crime, poverty, and stress of all forms.

19. The need for labor will increase, thus all members of society will have productive roles. Unemployment will decline, women and older Americans will continue to take a more active part in the labor force.

20. There will be less emphasis on higher education, with more education of individuals in the trades and crafts. There will be less need for specialists of all kinds and education will shift emphasis to a more general education, with less need to prepare the student to fit into a very complex social system.

21. The family unit will become of greater importance, with smaller scale social systems such as blocks and neighborhoods having primary importance over national and global systems. The trend will be for more regionalization of culture rather than the reverse that has been predicted.

22. As the negative aspects of population density interactions decrease, there will be less need for the professions that are trained to deal with these problems, and more of a need for professions that deal with organizing populations in productive tasks.

23. Politics will take on a more regional character, with more participation by individuals in the governing of local populations. In general there will be less of a need for complex laws to protect the "common good".

A good exercise for the reader might be to imagine that you were a part of the group of businessmen who participated in the Forum. How would you have responded to each of the five questions? What significant contribution could you make to the overall summary?

REFERENCES AND RECOMMENDED READING

CHAPTER I

1. Douglas, Marjory Stoneman, *Florida: the Long Frontier*. New York: Harper and Row, Pub.; 1967.
2. Tebeau, C.W., *A History of Florida*. coral Gables: University of Miami Press; 1971.
3. Sprague, G.T., *The Florida War*. (Quardricentennial Edition of the Floridana Facsimile Reprint Edition), Gainesville: University of Florida Press; 1964.

CHAPTER II

1. Craighead, F.C., Sr., *Trees of South Florida* (3rd Printing). Coral Gables: University of Miami Press; 1974.
2. Douglas, M.J., *The Everglades: River of Grass*. New York: Rinehart & Co., 1947.

CHAPTER III

1. Bathurst, R.G.C., *Developments in Sedimentology: Twelve Carbonate Sediments and Their Diagenesis*. New York: Elsevier Pub. Co.; 1971.
2. Moore, Lalicker, and Fischer, *Invertebrate Fossils*. New York: McGraw-Hill, Inc.; 1952.
3. Schuchert, Chas., *Historical Geology of the Antillean-Caribbean Region*. New York: Hafner Pub. Co.; 1968.
4. Shrock and Twenhofel, *Principles of Invertebrate Paleontology*, 2nd Ed. (International Series in the Earth and Planetary Sciences: Geography). New York: McGraw-Hill, Inc.; 1953.

CHAPTER IV

1. Calder, N., *The Restless Earth*. New York: Viking Press; 1972.
2. Griswald, O., *The Florida Keys and the Coral Reef*. Miami: The Graywood Press; 1965.
3. Sloane, M.E., "Protecting a National Treasure", N.O.A.A. Quarterly Magazine, Vol. VI, No. 2, April, 1976. Washington, D.C.: Gov't Printing Office.
4. Windhorn and Langley, *Yesterday's Florida Keys*. Miami: E.A. Seaman Pub. Co.; 1974.

CHAPTER V

1. Arn, E.F., *Oil for Today...and Tomorrow.* Kansas City: The Interstate Oil Compact Commission;—
2. Means, J.A., "Southern Florida Needs Another Look", *The Oil and Gas Journal,* (pp 212-222) Jan. 22, 1977.
—"'Oil Prospecting, Well Drilling, and Production", *FloridaGeological Survey Biennial Report,* No. 6, (18-22) 1943-44.

CHAPTER VI

1. Anderson and Hughes, *Hydrology of Three Sinkhole Basins in SW Seminole County, Florida.* Tallahasee: Bureau of Geology; 1975.
2. Smith and Griffin, *The Geothermal Nature of the Floridan Plateau.* Tallahassee; Bureau of Geology; 1977.

CHAPTER VII

1. Browder, Littlejohn, and Young, *The South Florida Study.* Gainesville; Center for Wetlands, University of Florida; 1977.
2. —' *Kissimme River Restudy, Florida.* Vero Beach: U.S. Fish and Wildlife Service, Division of Ecological Services; 1979.
3. —' *Wetlands of the United States.* Washington, D.C.:Gov't Printing Office; 1984.
4. —'*Central and Southern Florida Kissimmee River, Florida.* Jacksonville: U.S. Corps of Engineers, Jacksonville District; 1984 (Draft).

CHAPTER VIII

1. Morton, Julia, *Wild Plants for Survival in South Florida.* Hurricane House Pub., Inc.; 1968.

CHAPTER IX

1. Bradkorb, P., *The Avifauna of the Bone Valley Formation.* Tallahassee: Bureau of Geology; 1985.
2. Pirkle, Yoho, & Hendry, *Ancient Sea Level Stands in Florida.* Tallahassee: Bureau of Geology; 1970.
3. Scott and MacGill, *The Hawthorn Formation of Central Florida.* Tallahassee: Bureau of Geology, 1981.
4. —' *Habitat Reclamation Guide.* Tallahassee; The Florida Game and Freshwater Fish Commission; 1985.
5.—' *Billions of Years Ago.* Lakeland: Florida Phosphate Council;—.

CHAPTER X

1. Manucy, A., *The Houses of St. Augustine 1565-1821.* Tallahassee: Rose Printing Co. (for the St. Augustine Historical Society); 1978.
2. Waterbury, J.P., Ed., *The Oldest City.* St. Augustine: The St. Augustine Historical Society; 1983.

INDEX

Acid (also Acidity)—
29,30,31,40,67,94,99*
Acid, Amino—94,99*
Aggregate—106,110*
Ais Indian—See Indians, Ais
Algae—37,39,42*
Alkaline (also Alkalinity, Base)—
94,99*
Amino acid—See Acid, Amino
Amoeba—56,60*
Anastasia Island—106,107,110*
Aquifer—68,69,70,71*,75,83
Aragonite—41,42*
Artesian Zone—68,69,70,71*
Axis of Florida—69,71*,96,99

-B-

Benthos—38,42*
Biscayne Aquifer—32,33*
Bone Valley—96,99*
Bone Valley Formation—
92,93,96,99*
Boulder Zone—69,70,71*
Bryozoa—37,39,42*
Bryozoan Limestone—See Limestone,
Bryozoan

-C-

Calcareous Algae—56,57,58,60*
Calcareous Limestone—See
Limestone, Calcareous
Calcareous Structure—
45,51,56,57,60,67,71
Calcite—40,41,42*,95,96,99
Calcium Carbonate—See Calcite
Calcium—94,95,99*
Caloosa Indian—See Indian, Caloosa
Capron Trail—See Trail, Capron
Castillo de san Marcos—
104,106,107,108,110*
Catalyst—40,42*,94,99
Causeway—22,24*,46,48,51
Cay—45,46,50,51*
Chitinous Covering—56,60*

Clay—96,97,99*,107
Confining Layer (of Limestone)—
67,69,71*
Conglomerate—94,100*
Connate Water—54,60*
Coral—37,39,42*,45,50
Coralline Algae—See Calcareous
Algae
Coral Rock—46,51*
Coquina Rock—106,107,108,110*
Cretaceous—See Geological Time
Period
Crustacian—53,57,58,60*
Cuttings—63,71*
Cypress Strand—53,60*,77

-D-

Detritus—30,33*
Deep Well Injection—70,71*
Digestion—94,100*
Dolomite—See Limestone,
Dolomitic

-E-

Ecosystem—31,33*,49,58,60
Eocene—See Geological Time Period
Estaurine Habitat—56,92,100*

-F-

Fauna—19,25*,
29,33,45,51,58,60,80,83
Firebreak—85,91*
Flora—22,25*,29,33,45,
51,58,61,66,72,80,83,90,91
Floridan War—17,24,25*
Floridan Aquifer—68,69,70,72*
Food Chain—94,100*
Foraminifer—39,42*,55,56,61
Fort Brooke—16,24*
Fort Christmas—78,83*
Fort Dallas—18,24*
Fort Drum—18,24*,78
Fort Jupiter—18,24*

NOTE: Words and phrases listed in the Index and marked with an asterisk (*) indicate the page on which the word or phrase is described.

Fort Lloyd—18,25*
Fort Meade—92,100*
Fort Pierce—18,25*
Fort Vinton—18,25*
Fort Taylor—18,25*
Fossil—37,43*,
  50,55,56,58,92,93,100

-G-

Genetic Material—94,100*
Geologist—92,100*
Geological Time Period
  Cretaceous—53,55,56,57,58,60*
  Eocene—68,72*
  Mesozoic—55,61*
  Miocene—36,37,38,40,43*,
    68,72
  Pleistocene—37,43*
  Pre-Cambrian—56,61*
Geothermal Energy—69,72*
Giant Tun—36,43*
Glacial Period—47,51*,58
Granite—54,61*
Guano—94,101*

-H-

Hammock—20,21,25*,
  29,33,88,91
Hawthorn(e) Formation—96,101*
Highlands (of Florida)—68,69,72*
Hogback—27,28,30,32,33*
Hotsprings—69,70,72*
Humus—29,33*
Hydrologic Cycle—76,83*

-I-

Indian Tribal Names
  Ais—19,24*
  Caloosa—45,46,50,51*
  Miccasukee—53,61*
  Seminole—18,19,21,25*
  Timucua—105,106,111*
Indigenous Plants—89,91*
Insectivore—58,61*
Interglacial Period—47,51*,58

-L-

Land Pebbles—92,96,101*
Lauderdale Trail—See Trail,
  Lauderdale
Leaching—40,41,43*
Lime-producing Algae—See
  Limewort Algae
Limestone (Limerock)—
  29,30,34,37,
  39,40,41,43,54,55,57,58,61,65,
  67,68,69,70,72,76,83,95,96,
  101,107,110
Limestone, Types of
  Bryozoan—32,33*,37,42
  Dolomitic—95,96,100*
  Oölite—107,110*
  Phosphitic—See Phosphate Rock
  Pleistocene—See Geological Time
    Period Pleistocene
  Tamiami—37,44*
Limerock—
Limewort (Lime-producing Algae)—
  37,39,56,61 (See Alcareous Algae)
Lithification—40,43*
Lost Circulation—63,64,69,72,
  (See Cuttings)

-M-

Magnesium—94,95,96,101*
Marl—29,34*,107
Mesozoic—See Geological Time
  Period
Miccasukee Indian—See Indian,
  Miccasukee
Micrite—40,43*
Microcrystalline Ooze—See Micrite
Midden—45,51*
Miocene—See Geological Time
  Period
Mineral Springs—See Hot Springs
Muck Pond—29,34*

-N-

Neo-Limestone—40,43*
Nitrogen—94,101*

126

Nucleus—94,101*

-O-

Old Military Trail—See Trail,
  Old Military
Oölite—See Limestone, Oölite
Overburden—96,97,101*

-P-

Paleontologist—50,61*,92,102
Peat—29,34*
Percolate—29,34*,40,43,67,72
Periphyton—31,34*
Phosphate—92,94,95,96,97,102*
Phosphate Rock—95,96,102*
Phosphitic Limestone—See
  Phosphate Rock
Phosphorous—94,96,102*
Photon—48,51*
Piedmont—66,72*
Plankton—57,61*,94,102
Pleistocene—See Geological
  Time Period
Pleistocene Limestone—
  See Limestone, Pleistocene
Polyp—45,48,52*
Portland Cement—106,107,110*
Potassium—94,102*
Pre-Cambrian Age—See Geological
  Time Period
Precipitate—41,43,67,72*
Preservation Zone—32,34*
Protein—94,102*
Protoplasm—57,58,61*
Protozoa—39,43*
Pseudomorph—37,38,40,43*

-Q-

Quicklime—106,111*

-R-

Recharge an Aquifer—70,72*,79
Respiration—94,102*
Riprap—46,52*

River-pebbles—92,96,102*
Rock Reef—27,28,30,31,32,34*
Rookery—93,94,102*
Rustid—56,57,61*

-S-

Sand—96,97,102*,106
Sandstone—55,61*
Savannah—58,61*
Scuba—67,73*
Second Indian Wars—See Florida
  War
Sedimentary Rock—39,43*
Seminole Indian
Silt—97,103*
Sinkhole—63,64,65,67,69,70,73*
Slough—20,84,85,91*
Solution Hole—29,35*
Speelunking—67,73*
Sponge—37,43*
Springs, Hot, Mineral
Stalactite—67,73*
Stalagmite—67,73*
Stratographic Change—58,61*
Stratographic Entrapment—55,62*
Strip Mining—96,103*
Subaerial Environment—40,44*
Sub-marine Environment—40,44*
Synthesis—94,103*

-T-

Tabby—
  104,105,106,107,108,109,111*
Tamiami Limestone—See Limestone,
  Tamiami
Timacua Indian—See Indian,
  Timacua
Trails in Florida
  Capron—18,24*
  Ft. Pierce–
    Lauderdale—17,18,25*
  Old Military—
    17,18,19,20,22,25*
Tree Island—27,29,30,32,35*